Financial Manag

This text has been specifically designed and written in a readable and user-friendly style. It takes as its main theme the role played by the financial manager in obtaining and investing funds within an organization.

The book is intended to help the reader to appreciate and understand the sources of finance available and their respective merits; the considerations which need to be taken into account and the techniques which can help when making investment decisions; evaluating performance via working capital management, dividend policy and the valuation of shares; budgetary control and strategic management; mergers and takeovers, and an introduction to foreign exchange management.

Financial Management has clearly defined objectives for each chapter, step-by-step examples, self-check assessments, instant feedback and concise chapter summaries. It also contains a variety of approaches with a helpful glossary of terms and will be suitable for business and non-business undergraduates, MBA students and managers who require an insight into the subject which is presented in a clear and concise format.

Leslie Chadwick has written widely on accounting and finance. His works include articles for leading business and professional journals as well as several books. He has many years' experience of teaching both students and managers. He is currently a Lecturer in Accounting and Finance at Bradford University Management Centre. **Donald Kirkby** is a freelance lecturer in financial management and accounting and currently holds visiting lectureships at various universities. He has written numerous articles for professional journals and is currently an accredited tutor for the Sports Council.

Elements of Business Series
Series editor: David Weir
University of Bradford Management Centre

This important new series is designed to cover the core topics taught at MBA level with an approach suited to the modular teaching and shorter time frames that apply in the MBA sector. Based on current courses and teaching experience, these texts are tailor-made to the needs of today's MBA student.

Other titles in the series:

Management Accounting
Leslie Chadwick

Business and Society
Edmund Marshall

Business and Microeconomics
Chris Pass and Bryan Lowes

Managing Human Resources
C. Molander and J. Winterton

Forthcoming:

Business and Macroeconomics
Chris Pass, Bryan Lowes and Andrew Robinson

Managerial Leadership
Peter Wright

Financial Management

Leslie Chadwick and Donald Kirkby

London and New York

First published 1995
by Routledge
11 New Fetter Lane, London EC4P 4EE

Simultaneously published in the USA and Canada
by Routledge
29 West 35th Street, New York, NY 10001

© 1995 Leslie Chadwick and Donald Kirkby

Typeset in Garamond by Pure Tech Corporation, Pondicherry, India

Printed and bound in Great Britain by Mackays of Chatham PLC

British Library Cataloguing in Publication Data
A catalogue record for this book is available from the British Library

Library of Congress Cataloguing in Publication Data
Chadwick, Leslie, 1943–
    Financial management/Leslie Chadwick and Donald Kirkby.
        p.   cm. — (Element of business)
    Includes bibliographical references and index.
    1. Business enterprises—Finance.   2. Corporations—Finance.
I. Kirkby, Donald.   II. Title.   III. Series.
HG4026. C446   1994   94–4 4801
658. 15—dc20   CIP

ISBN 0–415–11066–1 (hbk)
ISBN 0–415–11067–X (pbk)

Contents

Section VI Other topics

Figures and tables

FIGURES

TABLES

Preface

This book is written with a view to providing a text that is less demanding than the major texts on financial management. However, it does attempt to go beyond simply providing an introduction to the subject and should prove to be beneficial in meeting the needs of managers, executives and students who require an insight into the subject beyond an initial level of understanding.

It has therefore been specially designed and written to fill particular gaps existing within the publishing market. Thus, the principal objectives aim to 'bridge the gap' and to provide managers, executives and students with:

- A basic introduction to, and a first course text on financial management. Many other very good texts on the subject are available but tend to be too advanced, too theoretical and too high a level from the viewpoint of providing an elementary introduction to the subject.
- A book that is ideal for use on a *one-semester* course or a *modular course* of between 8 and 15 weeks' duration. Many of the existing texts are designed for use over a longer period, such as a full academic year.
- A text that is readable, understandable, enjoyable, clear and concise, and above all '*user friendly*'. This, it is hoped, has been achieved by adopting the principle of 'teaching by objectives', a 'user-friendly' style of writing, in addition to:
    —clearly stated chapter objectives;
    —step-by-step examples;
    —a selection of self-assessment questions and *instant feedback* via the suggested answers/appropriate sections of the chapters within the text;
    —a variety of approaches to enable it to convey its message, hopefully in an interesting way;
    —concise chapter summaries;
    —suggestions for further reading.

WHO CAN BENEFIT FROM USING THIS TEXT?

The text should be of interest to any manager, executive or student who is encountering the subject for the first time or to help support their learning programmes. It should be of particular interest to students undertaking a foundation level course in financial management on an MBA, and on a degree course or BEC HNC/HND course in business and non-business related areas. The book should also prove useful to those people who are studying via a distance learning programme, such as those offered by the Open College and Open University because of its open learning, user-friendly style.

The five appendices provide an insight into the UK tax system, financial numeracy, discount tables, suggested answers to certain self-check questions and a glossary of some of the terms used.

ACKNOWLEDGEMENT

Thanks are due to CIMA (Chartered Institute of Management Accountants) for permission to reproduce certain portions, as indicated within the text, from L. Chadwick and R. Pike *Management and Control of Capital in Industry*, CIMA (1985).

Leslie Chadwick, MBA, FCCA, Cert. Ed.
Don Kirkby, MSc., FCA, ATII, Cert. Ed.

Section I

Overview

Introduction

This text is taking as its main theme the role played by the financial manager in obtaining and investing the funds within an organization and has been written using the funds flow model as its foundation. It also discusses performance evaluation and control and concludes with the associated topics of takeovers and foreign exchange management. The appendices include a brief introduction to the UK taxation system and aspects of financial numeracy in so far as these impinge on the topics contained within the text. There is a glossary of terms used, present value tables and a comprehensive index.

Financial management is a relatively new subject based on theories that have been established since the 1950s. The reader is introduced to some of these theories, though for a more comprehensive treatment reference should be made to the more detailed textbooks in this area. Financial decision-making draws on other subject disciplines such as economics, accounting, behavioural sciences, statistics and law.

The theory of business finance is based on the assumption that the managers of the business are seeking to maximize the wealth of the shareholders, and this is the approach adopted throughout this text. It is also assumed that businesses are operating in an efficient capital market whereby share prices accurately reflect the information available, and that managers are risk averse and will wish to be compensated for increased risk by requiring increased returns.

Chapter 1

The flow of funds

Objectives

When you have read this chapter you should be able to:

- identify the main financial decision-making areas;
- prepare funds statements from both historic and budgeted data;
- understand the effect of depreciation on the funds flow;
- understand how inflows and outflows of funds affect the resulting balance of cash in hand and at the bank.

FUNDS FLOW

There is a circular flow of funds, both into the organization (called inflows) and out of the organization (called outflows). The inflows consist of short-term funds, such as an overdraft obtained from the bank, medium-term funds, such as a loan obtained and repayable in say 5 years' time, and long-term funds, such as an issue of ordinary shares. The outflows can also be short term (e.g. an increase in stocks), medium term (e.g. repayment of a 5-year loan) and long term (e.g. the redemption of shares). The difference between the inflows and outflows in an accounting period is reflected in the change in the cash (and bank) position between the beginning and end of the accounting period.

The flow of funds approach highlights the three main decision areas involving finance namely:

- financing decisions;
- investment decisions;
- distribution decisions.

It also addresses the important issue of working capital management. This text considers these topics in some detail.

In order to trace the flow of funds over an accounting period, the differences between the opening balance sheet and the closing balance sheet are examined together with other relevant information, including details from the profit statement.

Let us examine the accounts of G. Guide Limited set out below.

Balance sheet	19X1 £000s	19X2 £000s
Fixed assets	70	90
Stocks	18	20
Debtors	12	9
Cash/bank	5	11
	105	130
Creditors	15	17
Issued capital	70	80
Retained earnings	20	33
	105	130

From the above information we are able to construct a statement showing the inflows and outflows of funds, which we call the funds statement.

Funds statement	£000s
Sources	
Net Profit (i)	13
Decrease in debtors (ii)	3
Increase in creditors (iii)	2
Issue of shares (iv)	10
	28
Uses	
Purchase of fixed assets (v)	20
Increase in stocks (vi)	2
	22
Change in cash/bank	6

Notes

(i) The retained earnings have increased by £13,000. Given no other information we assume that this is caused by the net profit generated during the year.

(ii) The debtors have reduced by £3,000 which means that extra funds have been received.

(iii) The creditors have increased by £2,000 which means that extra credit has been taken from the suppliers, a source of funds.

(iv) The share capital has increased by £10,000. Presumably more shares (e.g. ordinary shares) have been issued during the year.

(v) The fixed assets have increased by £20,000, which we assume has been caused by a purchase of additional fixed assets, e.g. a new machine, thus using funds.

(vi) The stock has increased by £2,000, which suggests the purchase of extra stock, e.g. raw materials.

The total sources exceed the total uses by £6,000, being the change in the bank/cash position.

Self-assessment 1.1

Henry Ltd Balance sheet	19X1 £000s	19X2 £000s
Fixed assets	40	50
Stocks	24	14
Debtors	14	18
Cash/bank	9	11
	87	93
Creditors	12	14
Issued capital	70	70
Retained earnings	5	9
	87	93

From the above information you are required to construct a funds statement for 19X2.

Depreciation

One of the problems when preparing a funds flow statement is to recognize that depreciation is a *non cash flow* item. The purchase of fixed assets is treated as a cash outflow and the sale of fixed assets is treated as an inflow. Depreciation involves no cash flow, either in or out; the cash outflow taking place when the cash is used to buy the fixed assets and the cash inflow when the asset is eventually sold. The profit entered on the funds statement as a source has however been reduced by the depreciation charged during the year. It is therefore necessary to add back the depreciation to the profit, for if no depreciation had been calculated, the profits would have been that much higher. Similar adjustments include profits and losses on sale of fixed assets, if any, which will have been used in the calculation of the net profit or loss for the accounting period. These adjustments simply arise out of the incorrect calculation of depreciation charged against profits over the life of the assets.

We will now examine the accounts of Gordon Ltd.

Balance sheets	19X3 £000s			19X4 £000s		
Fixed assets	Cost	Aggregate appreciation	Net	Cost	Aggregate depreciation	Net
Freehold Premises	100	–	100	114	–	114
Shop Fittings	10	8	2	12	9	3
Motor Vehicle	8	5	3	9	6	3
	118	13	105	135	15	120
Current assets						
Stock		110			154	
Debtors		10			6	
Cash/bank		9			1	
		129			161	
Current liabilities						
Creditors		7	122		5	156
			227			276
Issued capital			180			190
Retained earnings			47			86
			227			276

A motor vehicle which had cost £5,000 and which had been depreciated by £3,000, was sold during 19X4 for £1,000.

The funds statement will show:

			£000s
Sources			
Profit for the year			39
Depreciation: shop fittings	(ii)	1	
motor vehicles	(ii)	4	5
Loss on sale of motor vehicle	(iii)		1
Decrease in debtors			4
Proceeds from sale of motor vehicle			1
Issue of shares			10
			60
Uses			
Purchase of: Premises	(i)	14	
Shop fittings	(i)	2	
Motor vehicle	(i)	6	22
Increase in stock			44
Decrease in creditors			2	68
Decrease in cash/bank			8

This question is more involved than the last and it is necessary to prepare some working notes.

Workings

(i)

All at cost: (£000s):	Premises	Motor vehicles	Shop fittings
At the start	100	8	10
Sold		$-\dfrac{5}{3}$	
Additions	14	6	2
At the end	114	9	12

The additions are the missing figure, i.e. the difference between the opening and closing balances taking into account those fixed assets which were sold. This also applies to the calculation of depreciation. The details in italics indicate the interpretation of the missing figures, once we have entered all the known information.

(ii)

Provision for depreciation of:	Motor vehicles £000s	Shop fittings £000s
At the start	5	8
Sold	$-\dfrac{3}{2}$	
Depreciation for the year	4	1
At the end	6	9

(iii)

Sale of motor vehicle	£000s	
Vehicle at cost	5	as above
Less: depreciation	3	as above
Book value	2	
Proceeds	1	
Loss on sale	1	

Self-assessment 1.2

Why is depreciation entered with the sources of funds?

Dividends and taxation

There are two further problems which arise when we are dealing with company accounts, i.e. dividends and taxation. So far as the funds statement is concerned we must enter these items when *paid* as a use of funds. The workings are as follows:

	P&L appropriation A/C	
At the start	47	
Add: profit for the year		
(before tax)	44	
	91	
Less: tax	1	
dividends	4	5
At the end		86

	Dividends	Taxation
At the start (say)	3	2
Paid	3	2
	0	0
P&L Appropriation A/C		
(New provisions) (say)	4	1
At the end	4	1

As can be seen, the profit previously calculated as £39,000 is altered to £44,000. That is, out of profits of £44,000, taxation and dividends totalling £5,000 have been deducted. The amended funds statement will appear as follows:

Gordon Ltd			£000s
Sources			
Profit for the year			44
Depreciation: shop fittings		1	
motor vehicles		4	5
Loss on sale of motor vehicle			1
Decrease in debtors			4
Proceeds from sale of motor vehicle			1
Issue of shares			10
			65
Uses			
Purchase of: shop fittings	2		
premises	14		
motor vehicle	6	22	
Taxation paid		2	
Dividends paid		3	
Increase in stock		44	
Decrease in creditors		2	73
Decrease in cash/bank			8

Self-assessment 1.3

You are required to prepare a funds statement from the following information which relates to Scott Ltd:

Balance sheets	19X2 £000s	19X3 £000s
Issued share capital	75	95
Retained earnings	31	47
Long-term loan	40	50
Taxation	15	16
Proposed dividend	2	3
Trade creditors	32	43
	195	254
Plant and machinery at cost	100	185
Less: depreciation thereon to date	40	45
	60	140
Stock in trade	42	69
Trade debtors	29	27
Short-term investments	9	11
Cash at bank and in hand	55	7
	195	254

Notes

1 The proposed dividend for 19X2 was paid during the year together with an interim dividend for 19X3 amounting to £1,000.
2 The liability for taxation at the end of 19X2 was paid during 19X3.
3 Plant and machinery which had cost £40,000 and which had been depreciated by £39,000 was sold during 19X3 for £2,000.

Self-assessment 1.4

From the perusal of the solution to Scott Ltd, identify the financial decisions which have been taken by management during the year.

Projected funds flow

Where projected funds flow statements are prepared it is possible to identify problems as they emerge and allow the planner to overcome the problem in advance. This is where funds flow analysis is particularly useful. It represents the culmination of the whole budgeting process. The budgeted funds statement, which forms part of the finance budget, is prepared from the budgeted profit statement and budgeted balance sheets, rather than the historic financial statements. In addition, cash budgets can be prepared as part of the analysis.

Self-assessment 1.5

Robbins Ltd is planning its financial affairs for the forthcoming year and has decided to prepare a projected funds statement for 19X7. The balance sheet for 19X6 is shown below:

	£000s	
Plant and machinery at cost	96	
Less: aggregate depreciation	40	56
Motor vehicles at cost	24	
Less: aggregate depreciation	15	9
Stock in trade		22
Trade debtors		18
Cash at bank and in hand		12
		117
Trade creditors	15	
Proposed dividend	3	
Medium-term loan	40	
Share capital	29	
Retained earnings	30	117

The directors supply you with the following additional information about their plans for 19X7:

1   The net profit is expected to be £15,000.
2   A motor vehicle which cost £7,000 and had a written down value of £4,000 was to be sold for an estimated £3,000. A new vehicle was to be purchased for £11,000. Depreciation for the year was to be charged on the motor vehicles held at the end of the year at 20 per cent on cost.
3   Plant and machinery was to be bought for £17,000 and the total plant and machinery was to be depreciated by £13,000.
4   No taxation is payable during the year but an interim dividend of £1,000 is to be paid and a final dividend is proposed amounting to £2,000. Last year's proposed dividend will also be paid.
5   Stock in trade is to be increased to £30,000, trade debtors are to be reduced to £14,000 and trade creditors are to decrease by £7,000.
6   The loan will be reduced to £35,000.

You are required

1   to prepare a budgeted funds statement for the year ended 19X7;
2   to state the effect of the above proposals on the cash in hand and at bank.

Published cash flow statements

The published accounts of a company must include a cash flow statement prepared in accordance with the layout set out in FRS1. The above illustrations do not conform to that layout as the purpose of this text is to concentrate on financial planning rather than financial reporting. However, the workings shown will still provide the necessary figures for the published report, it is simply the layout which is different. The cash flow statement for Gordon Ltd, using the information in the funds statement above, would be presented as follows:

Gordon Ltd *Cash flow statement for the year ended 19X4*		
Net cash inflow from operating activities		8
Returns on investment and servicing of finance		
Dividends paid		(3)
Taxation paid		(2)
Investing activities		
Payments to acquire tangible fixed assets:		
Premises	14	
Shop fittings	2	
Motor vehicle	6	
Proceeds from sale of motor vehicle	(1)	
Net cash outflow from investing activities		(21)
Net cash outflow before financing		(18)
Financing activities		
Issue of shares	10	
Net cash inflow from financing		10
Decrease in cash and cash equivalents		8

Workings

The net cash inflow from operating activities is made up of the following items:

Profit for the year	44
Depreciation	5
Loss on sale of vehicle	1
Increase in stock	(44)
Decrease in debtors	4
Decrease in creditors	(2)
	8

Self-assessment 1.6

Using your solution to Self-assessment 1.3, Scott Ltd, prepare the cash flow statement required by FRS1.

SUMMARY

The funds statement contains details of sources and uses, which are of a short-, medium- or long-term nature. Funds flow analysis allows us to reconstruct from balance sheets and the linking profit statement important resource decisions involving financing, investment and distribution. It provides an insight into past decision-making and can be used as a basis for future decision-making, as it forms part of the finance budget.

Further reading

Chadwick, L. (1991) *Essence of Financial Accounts*, London: Prentice Hall.
Financial Reporting Standard (FRS) (1991) 1: *Cash Flow Statements, (1991)* UK: Accounting Standards Board.
Weston, J.F. and Copeland, T.E. (1988) *Managerial Finance*, London: Cassell.

Chapter 2

Profitability and liquidity considerations

This chapter aims to help you answer some of the questions which are often asked about profitability, liquidity, financial analysis and inter-firm comparisons.

Objectives

On completion of the chapter and the self-assessments which are provided, you should be in a position to:

- identify who invests in business and the type of investment which they are likely to make;
- explain why investors invest in business;
- understand why both profitability and liquidity are important to the success and survival of a company/organization.
- discuss the factors which affect the calculation of the profit (or loss), in particular via the accounting concepts, 'creative accounting' and 'window dressing';
- illustrate how the capital employed figure may be affected by those items which affect the calculation of the profit (or) loss and revaluations etc.;
- state, with examples, why it is very difficult to carry out a fair external inter-company comparison via ratio analysis.

WHO ARE THE INVESTORS?

Investors come in all shapes and sizes. Table 2.1 provides examples as to who some of them are, and the type of investment in which they may be involved. It also just goes to show what a wide range of investors there are.

WHY DO INVESTORS INVEST?

The principal reason why investors invest their funds is to put those funds to work so that they can earn a satisfactory return. However, there are many other reasons for investing their funds, some of which are:

- *Income.* Some investors may invest for the purpose of generating income. They may receive regular interest payments or have bought shares in a

Table 2.1 The types of investor and their investments

Type of investor	Examples of their investments
Individuals	*Direct* to family and friends via a loan or to a company via the purchase of shares *Indirect* to industry via unit trusts and insurance companies
A medium-sized company	Shares in other companies
Banks	Short-term and long-term loans, secured or unsecured
The treasury function of a company	Investing surplus cash on the 'money markets', e.g. overnight or one month
A holding company	Ordinary shares in subsidiaries, loans to subsidiaries
Merchant banks	Venture capital; also, multi-million pound loans, possibly via joining together with other banks/financial institutions
Self	Ploughing back the profits into the business, e.g. the retained earnings of a company.
Government and the European Union	Various grants/loan schemes

company which pays out a high proportion of its earnings as dividends. Thus, in the case of investing in ordinary shares, a company's dividend policy could play a significant part in attracting investors.

- *Capital gains.* Others may be attracted to purchase ordinary shares because of the prospect of making capital gains.
- *Security.* Banks for example may require security for some of the loans which they make. Some companies/institutions may invest in government stocks which in terms of receiving interest on the due dates and eventual repayment are a very low risk/relatively risk free. On the other hand certain investors who invest in the higher risk 'equity' (i.e. ordinary shares) shares, may restrict their investment/s to well established sound companies, even if it means they may get lower dividends and lower capital gains.
- *Control.* Ordinary shares may be purchased with a view to retaining or gaining control via the voting rights attached to those shares, or with a view to taking over the company concerned, e.g. as a subsidiary of a holding company.
- *A hedge against inflation.* An attempt, for example when interest rates are low and reasonably in line with the rate of inflation to generate a better return by investing in ordinary shares. Another example is where, when interest rates are high, making fixed interest loans provides a hedge against interest rates and inflation going down, and vice versa.
- *No choice!* Where employees belong to an employees' share scheme they may simply receive a certain number of shares in their own company.
- *Other reasons.* There can also be various other reasons for investing in certain companies, e.g. 'green issues' where investors prefer to invest in com-

panies/projects that take environmental factors into account or 'political' reasons, e.g. in connection with overseas investments.

FINANCIAL PERFORMANCE

The 'track record', i.e. the financial performance record of companies, is of particular importance to investors. Investors, as mentioned above, are very interested in getting a satisfactory return on their investment and also the security of their investment. They are therefore particularly interested in both profitability and liquidity.

Profitability, the return on capital employed (ROCE) which may also be called the return on investment (ROI), has been described as the real name of the business game. The capital invested has to be used productively. It is no use going for sales growth and an increased market share if, in the longer term, the return on capital employed is going to be poor. However, liquidity is also important. Liquidity is the ability to pay one's way. In the case of a business, this means the ability to remain solvent and to pay the debts as the debts become due. The section of the text which deals with working capital management is particularly concerned with this aspect.

It must be emphasized here, that profitability and liquidity do not go hand in hand. A company may be profitable and have a good return on capital employed, but may experience great difficulties or go out of business altogether because of liquidity problems!

The return on capital employed

What is profit (or loss)?

Profit is computed in accordance with various accounting concepts and principles. The amount may be affected by:

- The application of the concepts and principles, e.g. the depreciation policy and other accounting policies followed.
- 'Creative accounting', providing a picture of the profits which is not really the true position. For example, companies in certain industries such as the hotel and catering industry have been known to capitalize some of their interest payments. This results in higher profits and also higher capital employed.
- 'Window dressing', some companies may have sold a lot of stock at cost, which pushes up turnover, and then bought it back after their year end! This type of manoeuvre does affect the ratios which are computed, e.g. gross profit/sales, stock turnover etc.
- The way in which the company/organization finances its assets, e.g. outright purchase, leasing, renting, and hire purchase.

- The location of the business, e.g. having to pay higher rents for premises and higher wages and salaries to the labour force. This can have a very significant impact where companies set up plants in other countries.
- Capital structure, i.e. when the relative amounts of debt and equity financing can have dramatic effects on profits (losses), depending on trading conditions. For example, a 'highly geared' company, a company which has a high proportion of debt in the form of debentures or long-term loans is also high risk. If trading conditions are very bad, such companies still have to pay out large sums of interest to their debenture holders and long-term loan providers. To default in payment could lead to bankruptcy.
- The efficiency with which the company/organization is managed.

What is capital employed?

One quick calculation of the figure which may be described as 'capital employed' is, the shareholders' funds (i.e. share capital plus reserves) plus the long-term debt (i.e. debenture and/or long-term loans). The capital employed is also affected by the application of the concepts/principles, 'creative accounting', 'window dressing' and all of those other items listed above which affect the calculation of the profit (or loss). For example, anything which affects the profit (or loss) calculation automatically affects the retained earnings figure. If fixed assets are revalued, the amount of the revaluation affects both the fixed assets concerned and the reserves. If the revaluation is upwards, at a stroke, the capital employed increases!

Assessing profitability

$$\text{Profitability} = \frac{\text{The profit}}{\text{The capital employed}} \times 100$$

There are, however, several profitability ratios which can be used. Which one to use, depends upon who you are calculating it for and why they need to look at it. For example, the ordinary shareholders are particularly interested in what their return is, but the directors are possibly more interested in the productivity of all of the capital employed.

The ordinary shareholders would be interested in:

$$\frac{\text{Net profit } \textit{after} \text{ interest and tax (and preference dividends if any)}}{\text{Ordinary shareholders' funds (i.e. issued and paid up ordinary share capital plus reserves)}} \times 100$$

The directors/management would be interested in:

$$\frac{\text{Net profit } \textit{before} \text{ interest and tax}}{\text{Capital employed}} \times 100$$

Liquidity

Liquidity is concerned with the ability of a company/organization to meet its debts as and when the debts become due. This is why management should place a great emphasis on working capital management. Working capital management which includes inventory (stock) control, credit control and cash flow management will be dealt with in greater depth in Chapter 11.

Profitability v liquidity

The question as to which is the more important of the two can be answered as follows:

● A business needs to be profitable and to make a satisfactory return on the capital employed if it is going to attract investors and plough back profits.
● However, a business if it wishes to survive and stay in business must be able to pay its debts, e.g. creditors. If it is unable to meet its obligations it is quite likely that it will have to go into liquidation or be sold off.

Thus, it can be seen that they are both important and that a business needs to be profitable and sufficiently liquid to pay its debts. It is worth repeating that profitability and liquidity do not go in hand in hand, a company can be highly profitable but still experience severe cash flow problems.

The problems of comparing financial performance

Apart from situations where there have been significant changes in the accounting policies and/or revaluations etc. internal comparisons may be fair and reasonable. However, external inter-firm comparisons are a 'mine field'. It is very difficult to compare like with like. To do a fair comparison you really need to compare with a company which:

● is of a *similar size* in terms of turnover and the number of employees;
● has a similar product portfolio in the same industrial sector;
● makes up its accounts to the same year end, thereby covering the same period of time;
● follows similar accounting policies;
● finances its assets in a similar way and revalues them on a similar basis. For example, some companies may own their own land and buildings, others may rent theirs. Some companies may have revalued certain fixed assets, recently, some years ago or never revalued them!

Add to these the effects of 'window dressing', 'creative accounting' and 'off balance sheet financing', e.g. renting plant, machinery and equipment, and comparison is made even more problematical.

The use of ratio analysis does have to be performed with great care and thought and should where possible be used in conjunction with other data. The important thing about using accounting ratios is that they bring to light various questions, the answers to which can help managers manage more effectively, leading to improved profitability and a sound liquidity position.

SUMMARY

There are quite a number of organizations and institutions which provide business finance, ranging from an individual to the European Union (EU). They provide a wide range of finance, e.g. term loans, ordinary shares, multi-million pound loans etc. They invest, not just for the 'profit motive', i.e. to receive a return on their investment, but for various other reasons such as security and control.

The *calculation of the profit (or loss)* can be affected by many variables, e.g. the concepts and principles of accounting, the accounting policies, 'creative accounting', 'window dressing', the financing of assets, the location, and the company's capital structure. These items will also affect the *capital employed figure.* Anything which causes profit (or loss) to increase or decrease will, at the end of the day affect the retained earnings figure. Actions, such as the revaluation of fixed assets and/or the capitalization of loan interest will also affect the capital employed figure. In the case of a revaluation of fixed assets upwards, the reserves figure will increase. With the capitalization of interest, the profit will be higher, and this will impact on the retained earnings figure, see Table 2.2.

Table 2.2 The effect of a £400,000 revaluation of fixed assets or a £400,000 capitalization of loan interest

Fixed assets	+ £400,000
Reserves (or retained earnings as the case may be)	+ £400,000
Capital employed is	+ £400,000

- *Profitability*, the return on capital employed is important because investors will be attracted to invest because of it.
- *Liquidity* is also important as investors do like to feel secure and the company/organization concerned needs to be able to pay their way.

To be successful and survive a company/organization needs to be both profitable and liquid.

Comparing financial performance with other companies, even those within the same industrial sector may prove to be very difficult because of size, product portfolios, year ends, accounting policies etc. Thus, financial analysis needs to be conducted with care. On the face of it, it looks an impossible task. However, all one can do is to compare with those companies whose characteristics are as near as possible to those of one's own company.

To do nothing at all would be much worse; at least the accounting ratios do provoke numerous questions, and provide an indication of areas which management need to look at.

Self-assessments

When you have attempted each of these self check assessments, compare your attempt with the appropriate part of this chapter.

2.1 Give examples of five types of investor and state the type(s) of investment which they are likely to make.
2.2 Explain why investors are prepared to invest their funds in a business.
2.3 Discuss in an essay, the factors which affect the calculation of the profit (or loss) and the capital employed figure.
2.4 'Profitability is more important than liquidity', discuss.
2.5 Why is it difficult to carry out an external inter-company comparison which is fair and reasonable? Illustrate your answer with brief examples, as appropriate.
2.6 'Financial analysis is a "mine field".' Discuss in an essay, in terms of profitability, liquidity and inter-firm comparison. (Writing this essay could involve you in researching your answer by reviewing the relevant chapters in other appropriate texts.)

Further reading

Chadwick, L. (1991) *Essence of Financial Accounts*, London: Prentice Hall.
O'Gill, J. (1992) *Practical Financial Analysis*, London: Kogan Page.

Section II

Obtaining the finance

Chapter 3

External sources of business finance

Objectives

When you have completed working through this chapter you should be able to:

- understand and discuss the various short-, medium- and long-term sources of finance which are listed;
- appreciate why bank overdrafts can be regarded as long-term sources of finance;
- explain how the factoring of invoices works;
- know who the principal suppliers of funds are;
- describe why the issue of debentures increases the risk to the company concerned;
- list the characteristics of equity, preference shares and convertible loan stock and convertible debentures;
- recall the various factors which affect the ability of the company/organization to raise funds.

In everyday life capital is frequently used to describe money, but to the accountant capital means much more. To the accountant capital employed includes:

- share capital;
- retained profits; and
- loans and debentures.

The businessperson may well ask the question, 'Why is capital shown with the liabilities in the balance sheet? I thought it was my principal asset!' The answer to this question is that capital is an amount invested in the business by the proprietor, shareholder or other third party, and it does therefore represent a claim on the assets. Capital is increased by the portion of periodic income which is retained, i.e. ploughed back profits.

SOME FREQUENTLY ASKED QUESTIONS

Question: Where do I go to obtain capital?
Answer: A multitude of places, the list is endless.

Question: Which type of capital do I need?

Answer: It all depends upon how much you want and for how long you want it.

Question: How much will it cost me to borrow the money?

Answer: This will vary with each particular source, but one thing that is certain is that the charges will reflect the time span of the finance and the risk to the institution making the finance available. Remember that in addition to paying interest on loans there is also an obligation to repay the capital.

Question: How do I decide upon how long I need the capital for?

Answer: One way of doing this is to look at what you're using the capital for and matching it to the life of the asset or project.

The notion of *matching* the term/type of finance with the life of an asset or duration of a project is of practical application. The repayments of the capital and interest are being made out of the additional income supposedly generated as a result of employing the asset or taking on the project, e.g. company cars, which are to be replaced say every 2 or 3 years, could well be financed from short-term sources such as hire purchase or a short-term bank loan.

SHORT-TERM, MEDIUM-TERM OR LONG-TERM

The time scales shown in Figure 3.1 have been used for the purpose of our discussions within this chapter. However, you should note that what is short, medium or long, in practice will depend to a large extent on the size of the business and the nature of the industry. For example, in the aerospace industry long-term may be defined as over 20 years, medium term 7–15 years and short-term up to 7 years when it comes to the financing of assets/projects.

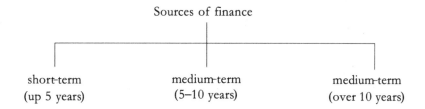

Sources of finance

short-term   medium-term   medium-term
(up 5 years)   (5–10 years)   (over 10 years)

Figure 3.1   Types of finance

Source: Chadwick, L. and Pike, R. (1985) *Management and Control of Capital in Industry*, London: CIMA.

Short-term sources of capital (up to 5 years)

Short-term capital can be utilized to provide cover for fluctuations in working capital, the financing of short-lived assets and transactions which are self-financing in the short term.

Bank overdrafts from the clearing banks and merchant banks offer a very flexible source of capital which is ideal for assisting in providing working capital. It must be noted, however, that a certain proportion of the working capital should be regarded as a *fixed investment* and financed from long-term sources of funds. Amounts can be repaid or withdrawn as and when appropriate. If the concern requires more on overdraft an increase can be negotiated quite speedily with the bank. In some cases the banks may ask for security or a guarantee. It is, however, a fact of business life, that many many organizations look upon and use their bank overdraft as a long-term source of funds.

For many companies their bank overdraft can be one of their highest forms of borrowing and also *secured* by a fixed or floating charge on their assets. More proof is provided by the banks themselves, in that they do try to get organizations to convert a certain proportion of their overdraft into a term loan. You should note that if an overdraft is treated as long term, then this will affect the liquidity ratios and gearing calculations.

Short-term loans are usually granted by the clearing banks and merchant banks for a particular purpose. The capital and interest is usually repaid in instalments at regular intervals. The interest charges may be fixed or variable. Depending upon the amount and the size and *track record* of the company concerned, the bank may require security. Loans are financial products, and if a business/company needs one (short, medium or long), it may be most advantageous to *shop around*. There are many different loan offerings around, for example:

- unsecured;
- secured;
- fixed rates of interest;
- variable rates of interest;
- with 'repayment holidays', e.g. no repayments for the first year.

Trade credit

One of the most frequently used sources of short-term finance is the trade credit provided by the suppliers of goods and services, i.e. creditors.

It is said,
That 'Honest Ed',
Buys goods on 90 days' credit,
In that time,
He sells them all, and
That's how he makes a profit.[1]

The time lag between the receipt of the goods and payment for them allows the company purchasing those goods to process/sell some or all of them. It is imperative that a company maintains a good working relationship with its suppliers. The support of sympathetic creditors in times of a cash flow crisis could prove vital to the survival of the company. However, where cash discounts are offered for prompt payment, this should not be ignored. It must be remembered that a discount of, say, $2\frac{1}{2}$ per cent for payment within 7 days of the invoice where normal settlement is, say, 45 days from the invoice date, amounts to a substantial effective annual rate (APR) of interest of around 24 per cent!

Bridging loans

These are usually used to cover the period between the exchange of contracts and the completion date for transactions involving the purchase or sale of property. The financial institutions tend to charge a rate of interest which is slightly higher than the rate that they charge on overdrafts, and may also require an arrangement fee.

Factoring

In this case the factoring/invoice discounting companies, in exchange for a fee, will provide immediate cash up to the value of around 75 to 85 per cent of the client company's invoices, i.e. trade debts. It can be applied to both home and overseas sales invoices. The factor may or may not be responsible for collecting the debts relating to the invoices which have been discounted, and this aspect will be reflected in the deal which is offered, e.g. the fees etc. Factors may also be employed to manage sales ledgers, and/or to provide credit ratings and/or to insure against bad debts.

'Accounts receivable' financing

It is also possible to arrange with certain financial institutions, such as merchant banks, hire purchase companies, etc., for them to provide a company with cash on a continuing basis by pledging debtors as security, as with invoice discounting.

Bills of exchange

The clearing banks, merchant banks, accepting houses and discount houses are all in the business of discounting bills of exchange. The seller of the goods and services drafts the bill, gets the purchaser to accept it, and then on its return from the purchaser the seller is able to obtain immediate payment by discounting the bill. The periods covered by bills of exchange tend to be from around 60 to 180 days. The use of this type of finance does help a business to convert a sale into cash very quickly after the goods have been dispatched. Charges will depend to a great extent upon the reputation of the buyer. Expert advice in drawing up a bill is available from the institutions who deal in this specialized type of finance.

Hire purchase

This tends to be quite an expensive method of buying assets. One must look very carefully at the effective rates of interest being charged. One must also be prepared to shop around. Some vendors may offer subsidized rates which may work out less expensive than short-term bank loans. (See also medium-term.)

Proposed dividends payable and accrued taxation

These are also valuable sources of short-term finance in that the company has the use of those funds for a particular period of time, i.e. there is a time lag between earning the profits and paying the tax or dividends.

Local and central government

The schemes are numerous, various and voluminous and one could write a book on this one aspect of financing. The offerings are constantly changing in name and shape. The accountant/financial manager should therefore ensure that he or she is up to date by obtaining information at regular intervals. From time to time there may be grants available for selected industries, e.g. hotels, tourism, manufacturing, small engineering, farming, microprocessing, microelectronics, software, computers, robotics, office and service industries, etc. Quite a number of firms may receive grants towards the cost of new buildings, plant and equipment if they are for use in specially designated development areas.

Where can we obtain information about grants?

A useful publication *Raising Finance*, by Clive Woodcock,[2] contains lots of useful addresses relating to government/EU (European Union) sources of finance. There is also the Department of Industry, local authorities, chambers of commerce and the EU itself.

Self-assessments 3.1

Before you progress any further it is perhaps wise to do a little recapitulation to ensure that you have been able to digest and understand the material. Prepare your answers in rough, and then compare them with the appropriate section of this chapter.

1 Why can it be useful to match the term/type of finance with the life of a project?
2 What proof is there that businesses tend to use their bank overdrafts as a long-term source of funds?
3 How did 'Honest Ed' become very rich?
4 What is meant by 'factoring of invoices'?

5   Who drafts a bill of exchange?
6   Why can hire purchase be less expensive than one would imagine?
7   How is it that proposed dividends payable and accrued taxation can be considered a short-term source of funds?

OTHER SOURCES

In addition to the sources mentioned there are many more, such as financing for exports, stocking loans and inter-company loans.

Medium-term sources of capital (5–10 years)

This type of finance is used mainly for providing additional working capital or for the purchase of fixed assets such as plant and machinery, fixtures and fittings, and office equipment, which have medium-term lives. Thus, the term of the finance is matched to the life of the asset, project or business venture. They may be also used for re-financing, e.g. converting the hard-core debt of an overdraft into a term loan.

Medium-term loans

A vast proportion of funds employed by manufacturing industry are now taken in the form of medium-term loans, quite probably as a direct result of the matching process. There are several sources from which this type of funding can be obtained, the principal ones are as follows:

● the clearing banks;
● merchant banks;
● finance houses;
● foreign banks;
● the EU.

The terms relating to interest charges and repayment vary considerably, providing the borrower with greater flexibility. Repayments can be scheduled in a number of ways, e.g.:

1   monthly, quarterly or half-yearly;
2   no repayments at all for the first one or two years, i.e. a 'repayment holiday';
3   interest only with the capital being repaid at the end of the term.

Such loans may be secured or unsecured depending upon the company's track record, e.g. profitability, size, credit worthiness and market expectations. The rates of interest charged are frequently linked to the LIBOR (London Inter-Bank Offered Rate). The company concerned may lose some degree of control over its affairs in that it may have to supply the financial institution concerned with information on a regular basis, e.g. cash flows, investment plans, etc.

Project loans

These are for specific projects which may have their repayment profiles linked to the cash flows expected from the project. These are available from the 'money market' made up of accepting houses, UK and overseas banks. *Call loans* are available from the 'money market' and enable the company to repay tranches of the loan during its life and to redraw as required.

Government schemes and EU schemes

Government (and EU) schemes come and go but may take the form of a *loan guarantee scheme*. This is a scheme in which the government guarantees a certain proportion of loans made by participating institutions, e.g. 70 per cent of the loan guaranteed in return for an annual premium of $2\frac{1}{2}$ per cent on the guaranteed portion of the loan. Support could also take the form of a *business expansion scheme*. Such a scheme is designed to encourage individuals to subscribe in new share capital in unquoted companies by providing them with tax relief on their investment. For example, investors may be allowed to deduct the cost of their investment, up to a statutory maximum, from their income tax, provided that the shares are held for a minimum of five years.

Debentures may be secured by fixed or floating charge. They appeal to investors who require a relatively risk-free fixed-return investment, e.g. pension funds. The risk to the company is increased because of the obligation to pay the interest irrespective of whether or not the company makes a profit.

Leasing is provided by leasing companies, finance houses, etc. It frees a company from having to find and repay a lump sum for a fixed asset, e.g. motor vehicles, machinery, office furniture and equipment. It can be argued that leasing of fixed assets does provide the company with a *hedge against obsolescence*, e.g. at the end of the lease a new and improved asset may be leased. The amounts paid for leasing machinery, furniture and equipment are allowable deductions in computing profits for UK tax purposes. Costs and conditions vary.

Hire purchase is usually used to buy a fixed asset, e.g. vehicles, fixtures and machinery. Hire purchase finance is provided by finance houses (a number of whom are subsidiaries of the clearing banks). The instalments paid at regular intervals (could be over the life of the assets, i.e. 'matching') are made up of capital and interest. It is important when assessing the cost of buying an asset on HP that the tax implications are clearly understood and taken into account.

Venture capital

This consists of share capital or loan finance provided by specialist institutions (e.g. the venture capital subsidiaries of commercial and merchant banks, government and EU sponsored organizations, pension funds, insurance companies, foreign institutions and private individuals), to finance new businesses and activities which may be classified as *high risk*, e.g. certain high-tech projects/ventures. The provision of funds from this source covers *small business start-ups* and *management buy-outs*.

Another source of venture capital is provided by *'corporate venturing'*. Although well established in the USA, it has been slow to take off in the UK. It involves a major company taking a small stake in a new/small company with or without the co-operation and involvement of a venture capital company. The assistance provided by the major company may involve the injection of more cash, and the sharing of ideas, skills and knowhow which may be of mutual benefit to both parties.

Self-assessments 3.2

Now see if you can answer the following self-check questions and then compare your attempted answers with the appropriate sections of this chapter.

1 Who are the principal suppliers of medium-term loans?
2 What does LIBOR mean?
3 How can an individual taxpayer benefit from a business expansion scheme?
4 To which type of investors do debentures appeal?
5 What is it about debentures that places the company which issues them under greater risk?
6 Why can a lease of equipment be regarded as 'a hedge against obsolescence'?
7 Which type of business assets can be bought on hire purchase in the short/medium term?
8 Who are the providers of venture capital?
9 What does 'corporate venturing' involve?

Long-term sources of capital (over 10 years)

Long-term sources of finance can be used to provide long-term assets, e.g. fixed assets such as buildings, for the purchase of investments, shares in a subsidiary and for the provision of the 'permanent' working capital.

Equity finance

This represents the *ordinary shares* which may be issued to shareholders, e.g. via the Stock Exchange to individual or institutional investors. There are a number of classes of ordinary shares with different rights as defined by a company's memorandum and articles of association. The latest Companies Act gives companies the power to issue redeemable ordinary shares, provided that certain conditions are complied with. The ordinary shares usually have voting rights, and the holders receive:

● dividends; and
● capital gains (or losses).

However, in the event of a company going into liquidation and winding-up, the ordinary shareholders are the last to be paid off.

Calls

Share capital which has not yet been called up gives a company the added flexibility as to the amount and the timing of future inflows from this source. It should be remembered that once all the cash has been received from an issue of shares, the buying and selling of those shares on the open market does not provide any new finance for the company whose shares are being traded.

Preference shares

The preference shares usually have no voting rights unless their dividends are in arrear. They tend to be redeemable and attract a fixed rate of dividend. They may be:

- cumulative or non-cumulative; and
- participating or non-participating;

as regards dividends.

Long-term loans

Long-term loans are provided by:

- the clearing banks;
- merchant banks;
- finance houses, etc.

Syndicated loans are available via the 'money market' and have been developed to provide the huge amounts required by multinational companies and public corporations. *A number of banks come together to provide the facility with the syndicate leader.* The terms relating to repayment of capital and interest are varied and again the company may have to surrender some of its independence, e.g. *a loan with strings attached* such as the provision of information, the provision of security, and the vetting of investment plans, etc.

Mortgage loans with repayment periods ranging from around 10 to over 30 years are available from insurance companies, finance houses and pension funds.

Debentures or loan stock

(See debentures already described above.)

Convertible loan stock (and convertible debentures)

Convertible loans/debentures tend to be offered at a lower rate of interest (at the time of issue), because of their convertibility into ordinary shares. The holder has the option to convert into ordinary shares between the specified dates at a pre-determined share price. The benefits to the company of being able to issue convertibles, are:

- the interest payable (i.e. the cost of servicing the loan) tends to be lower than the going rate of interest on debentures, loan stock etc. at the time of issue;
- the company does not have to find a lump sum in the future to repay the debenture holders/loan stock provider;
- on conversion, the company is freed from the obligation to pay interest on the debentures/loan stock.
- However, if and when the holders do convert, the company could experience some *loss of control* because of the voting rights attached to the new ordinary shares.

Another problem which may arise on conversion is the '*dilution of earnings*'. This means that the earnings per share goes down as a result of there being an increased number of shareholders, even though the company no longer has to pay the interest on the convertible debentures/loan stock. The company's share price is also likely to go down. From a shareholder's point of view, they can stick with the convertible debentures/loan stock and carry on receiving interest, or convert when the due dates are reached and benefit from any capital gains on the ordinary shares and receive dividends.

Sale and lease back

This highly specialized type of finance usually involves the sale of land and buildings to an insurance company which are then leased back for a term of years, e.g. 25 years. This method enables an organization to provide the large amount needed to finance, say, the construction of a new building.

Government sources

As mentioned earlier, there are numerous governmental sources of finance, which are essentially long-term.

European Union (EU)

Funds are also available from the EU, e.g. via the European Investment Bank (EIB).

Self-assessments 3.3

Now attempt these self-check assessments and compare your attempt with the relevant portion of this chapter.

1   What is 'equity finance'?
2   List the characteristics of ordinary shares.
3   Explain what 'calls' are in relation to ordinary share capital.
4   List the key features of preference shares.
5   Which companies may need to obtain a 'syndicated loan'?
6   What is meant, when we talk about 'loans with strings attached'?
7   How can the issue of convertible loan stock benefit a company?
8   What are the drawbacks from the company's point of view of issuing convertible loan stock?
9   Why is it that investors are prepared to invest in convertible loan stock?

Other alternatives to borrowing funds from external sources

Sub-contractors

Sub-contractors can save the company having to borrow to purchase expensive premises and equipment and may also relieve it from having to acquire and hold certain stocks of raw materials, fuels, work-in-progress and finished goods. In addition to not having to fund certain fixed and current assets, the company can make savings on overheads and the costs associated with the holding of stocks and borrowing funds. The sub-contractor has to remunerate its own work force and stand the costs associated with employing them, e.g. personnel and welfare, training, recruitment and selection etc. As with leasing, it can be said that this alternative approach to the financing of assets can be described as a hedge against obsolescence. The risk of plant, machinery and equipment becoming obsolete rests fairly and squarely upon the shoulders of the sub-contractor.

Renting or hiring of fixed assets

The idea here is that the company/organization does not have to find a lump sum. The financing of the rental or hire charge comes out of earnings for each period. Fixed assets employed in this way, become self-financing, i.e. as they are used they generate revenue to provide funds to pay the rental/hire charges. They also, provide a hedge against obsolescence. Thus, where technological change is a distinct possibility it could be worthwhile considering this option.

Factors which may affect a company's ability to raise finance

The type, the term, the timing and the amount of finance required will depend upon a number of factors, such as:

● the *purpose* for which it needs the finance, e.g. buying property;
● *the stage that the company has reached in its financial lifecycle*, as illustrated by the amended Boston Matrix, Figure 3.2.

Cash

Star	Problem child

Growth

Cash cow	Dog

Figure 3.2 The amended 'Boston Matrix'

The star

The star, lots of growth, lots of cash: it is just like a magnet when it comes to attracting finance. Of the four categories it is the most likely to be able to issue convertible loan stock or convertible debentures.

The problem child

The problem child, has lots of growth, but needs cash. It is quite likely that it will have a low percentage payout when its dividend policy is reviewed.

The cash cow

The cash cow has no growth, but lots of cash. It does not need to raise much new finance.

The dog

The dog will find it more difficult to raise finance and will no doubt find it has to pay higher rates of interest if it wishes to borrow.

- *The track record* of the company in terms of financial performance and how it has conducted its affairs, e.g. its bank account, both matter. A start-up 'problem child' with no track record may find it difficult in its early years to attract new investment.
- The *value of fixed assets* which can if necessary be pledged as *security* for a loan or debentures.
- The need to retain *control*, e.g. issuing more ordinary shares, could bring about the loss of a controlling interest.
- *Market expectation* is difficult to assess, but is a factor which does play a part in attracting investment, in the form of share capital or loan capital.

- *The firm's current financing mix* in terms of its *gearing*, i.e. the debt to equity relationship. If it is highly geared it may find it difficult to issue more debt, e.g. debentures or long-term loans.
- The establishment of *good working relationships* with the providers of finance, e.g. by keeping them informed of developments within the company.
- The cost of the finance.
- Legal considerations, e.g. the amount of the authorized share capital.

Finally, you should note that the provision of finance is a 'system of costs and risks'. The higher the risk the more the company/organization has to pay for new funds, e.g. 'the dog' mentioned earlier.

SUMMARY

There are many different types of finance available for the short, medium and long terms, for example:

Short-term

- bank overdrafts;
- loans;
- trade credit;
- bridging loans;
- factoring;
- bills of exchange;
- hire purchase;
- proposed dividends;
- accrued taxation;
- government/EU.

Medium-term

- loans;
- government;
- debentures;
- leasing;
- hire purchase;
- venture capital;
- government/EU.

Long-term

- equity, i.e. ordinary shares;
- preference shares;
- loans;

- convertible loan stock;
- convertible debentures;
- sale and leaseback;
- government/EU.

Many of the above can be described as 'financial products', and it must be said that there are many different offerings about. Thus, the financial manager needs to shop around to see what is available and which is the most suitable to meet the financial needs of the company/organization. Other alternatives to borrowing funds include the rent or hire of fixed assets, e.g. property, machinery etc. or employing sub-contractors.

Factors which affect a company's ability to raise finance are:

- the *purpose* for which it needs the finance;
- the stage it has reached in its financial lifecycle;
- its track record;
- the security available;
- control;
- market expectations;
- its financing mix and 'gearing';
- relationships with the providers of finance;
- the cost;
- legal considerations.

> *Finance* = A system of costs and risks

Further assignments

These require you to apply and use your knowledge of business as well as reviewing other appropriate literature.

Suggested essays

1   Explain briefly the advantages and disadvantages to a company of using:
- a bank overdraft;
- trade credit (i.e. finance from creditors);
- the factoring of invoices;
- debentures;
- venture capital;
- ordinary shares;
- convertible loan stock.

2   Describe *four* alternative ways of financing assets other than by borrowing a lump sum at the outset.

3   In your own words, explain briefly how the company's position in its own financial lifecycle affects its ability to raise funds (using the descriptions of companies given in the amended 'Boston Matrix', see Figure 3.2).

4   You have to raise a further £10m for your company. How would you go about this. Which forms of finance would you recommend, and why?

Notes

1   Written by Leslie Chadwick, inspired by the story of 'Honest Ed', the man who re-opened the Old Vic Theatre in 1983.
2   Woodcock, C. (1989) *Raising Finance: the 'Guardian' Guide for the Small Business*, London: Kogan Page.

Further reading

Pike, R. and Neale, B. (1993) *Corporate Finance and Investment*, London: Prentice Hall.
Watts, B.K.R. (1994) *Business Finance* (M&E Handbook), London: Pitman.

Chapter 4

Internal sources of business finance

Objectives

When you have read this chapter you should be able to:

- appreciate why retained earnings are such an important source of finance;
- spell out what the benefits are of a strategy of surplus asset recognition and disposal;
- explain how becoming more efficient can improve the amount of finance available;
- question the need for investing in new assets and list some of the non-financial factors which also need to be taken into consideration.
- describe what management can do to improve inventory control (stock control);
- explain ways in which credit control can become more effective;
- appreciate the roles that can be played by bankers and auditors.

INTRODUCTION

One of the major sources of UK business finance is the *profits that are ploughed back* and invested in the business in working capital and assets, i.e. the *retained earnings* (undistributed profits). *Depreciation* itself is not a source of funds, but a means of retaining the funds generated by operations.

However, in addition to the finance provided by ploughing back profits, management may be able to *sell off surplus assets*, and generate additional finance simply by *improving the efficiency* of the various business functions.

- 'If interest rates were reduced manufacturing industry would invest more in plant and machinery.'
- 'Industry needs to invest more in re-equipping itself.'

The above statements reflect an attitude which tends to suggest that the only way to improve efficiency and productivity is by the introduction of new capital equipment. Often this is true, but in other cases it could be well worth investing in organization. Improved organization, communications, co-operation and co-ordination could well reduce idle time, e.g. waiting time, training new operatives, etc. Improved methods could also bring about better utilization of the capital already employed.

- 'Let's see the bank manager about an increase in the overdraft.'
- 'I feel we must finance this by taking out a loan over 7 years.'

There is a great tendency when finance is required for a particular asset or project to look immediately to external sources. Companies, however, do have hidden sources of finance which can improve their cash flow, such as surplus assets, cash to be released by improved stock control and improved credit control. All branches of management should be concerned with improving the productivity of the capital employed. It is therefore of prime importance that all business functions work together in harmony. The article which now follows, 'Buried treasure'[1] provides you with a concise but detailed appraisal of the sources of internal finance.

BURIED TREASURE

Treasure! Where?

Management tend to seek new funds instead of making better use of those which they already have. A firm's balance sheet is rather like a treasure map, in that it frequently contains hidden capital, because the management and control of fixed assets and working capital has been neglected. Finance is an extremely scarce and expensive commodity and should be used in exactly the same way as any other scarce resource, that is, with efficiency. It is of utmost importance that management are actively involved and concerned with cash flow and the productivity of capital.

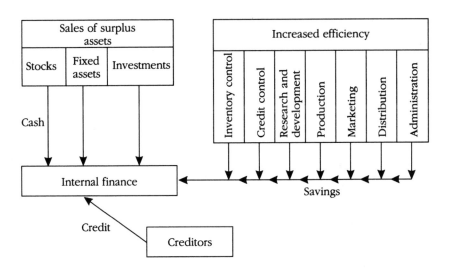

Figure 4.1 Internal finance from fixed assets and working capital, and increased efficiency

Efficient management and control of fixed assets and working capital can help to generate a considerable amount of finance (see Figure 4.1).

So where are all these sources of finance which are hidden in the balance sheet?

Surplus assets

A strategy of surplus asset recognition and disposal is quite likely to: make a substantial improvement in cash flow; reduce overheads; increase the space available for production, storage of inventory and administration; and improve machine utilization. Fixed assets and current assets, such as stock, represent capital tied up in physical resources. If these resources are not being used, the productivity of capital is bound to suffer. In addition to this they are also tying up funds which could be used elsewhere in the organization.

Case study

Following a very careful review of all their business assets, Wik Ltd discovered that certain machines, office equipment and inventory items were surplus to requirements. Buyers were found (finding a buyer does create a problem and should not be under-estimated) and the sale of the surplus assets realized £29,250 (cash flow improved, at a stroke). The space vacated by the sale of certain fixed assets was used for further company expansion (expanding without having to provide a new building). However, if the company had not needed the additional space created, it may have been possible to sell or sub-let all/some of it which would also bring about a reduction in overheads such as insurance and holding costs. The company did in fact experience a reduction in insurance as a direct result of the lowering of stock levels and plant values, and also achieved a saving of light, heat and power. They also managed to keep interest payments on new borrowings to a minimum. The investigation highlighted that certain machines were working at under-capacity. Getting rid of the surplus machines enabled the company to re-think their production methods and to improve the utilization of the remaining machines.

The replacement decision

In addition to the techniques for evaluating the investment of capital in new fixed assets, e.g. payback, discounted cash flow, it is of vital importance that the would-be investor obtains satisfactory answers to a wide range of questions, all of which may have significant implications for financial management. The questions to be considered could well include the following:

1   What do we need the machine for? Companies frequently purchase new machines with uncalled-for capability. Additional capacity and flexibility which may never ever be used ties up finance unnecessarily.

2   Will the supplier be prepared to allow a trade in allowance on the old fixed asset? 'Ask and ye shall find out.' The allowance could be much greater than the asset's scrap value.

3   Are there any competent sub-contractors? If so, the company's investment in fixed assets and inventory could be drastically reduced, not to mention the savings in overheads.

4   Is it possible to lease or hire the fixed asset? This would free the company from having to find an extremely large lump sum and could be regarded as 'a hedge against obsolescence'. Disposing of an obsolete fixed asset is not an easy task and could well result in a substantial loss. It could certainly prove much easier to cancel, complete or re-arrange a contract for the hire of an asset.

5   What is the opportunity cost? (i.e. the alternative forgone).

The replacement decision also involves consideration of a multitude of non-financial factors such as: availability of spares, frequency of maintenance, quality of after-sales service, standardization of fixed assets, delivery, reliability. However, all of these non-financial factors could well affect a firm's financial performance at some future date. Lost production would occur if a machine was out of use because of a breakdown or non-availability of spares. Standardization of fixed assets would reduce the need to significantly increase the stocks of spare parts, avoid the costs involved in re-training operatives, and ensure that the costs of routine maintenance are not permitted to escalate.

Inventory control

Stocks represent capital tied up in goods, therefore if stock levels can be reduced, the amount of capital can also be reduced. In addition to savings in interest payments and the freeing of storage space, the holding costs (e.g. storage, handling and re-handling, insurance) should be reduced. Reducing stock levels also lessens the risk of loss caused by obsolescence or deterioration. Inventories of raw materials, work-in-progress and finished goods, for many firms, represent a substantial investment. A small percentage reduction in inventory levels could, therefore, be responsible for savings amounting to several thousand pounds. It must be remembered that there is a trade-off between reducing stocks and the risk of causing production to come to a halt because of a 'stockout.'

What can inventory management do?

1   Management must review maximum, minimum and re-order stock levels at regular intervals and take seasonal fluctuations into account. This necessitates very close co-operation and co-ordination between all business

functions, e.g. finance, production and marketing. There is a great temptation on the part of the store-keepers to maintain high stocks in order to avoid production hold-ups.

2 *Pareto analysis* has been successful in improving inventory control and could prove to be a worthwhile exercise. 'Twenty per cent of your stock, could account for 80 per cent of your total inventory value.' Careful control of the 20 per cent, therefore implies that a vast proportion of the total stock valuation is subjected to greater scrutiny.

3 Firms have been known to order stock from suppliers which they could have obtained from within their own stores. This situation highlights the fact that a firm really does need a satisfactory *material classification system*. Such a system should be capable of ascertaining whether particular items exist, and their location.

4 *The regular delivery system* is worthy of consideration. Suppliers deliver components/materials at frequent intervals, which within a very short space of time are converted into finished goods and dispatched to customers. It can dramatically reduce a company's holding costs. This type of system is frequently referred to as JIT (Just In Time).

Credit control

The frequency with which cash flows into the firm from debtors and the avoidance of bad debts, in brief sums up what credit control is all about. The usual methods of credit control involve: credit screening, credit limits, aged analysis of debtors, systems of letters to slow payers, suspension of deliveries and discounts for prompt payment. However, it may be possible to achieve more effective credit control by the following means:

1 *Telephone contact.* A single telephone call may quickly establish the reason why a particular debtor has not paid. The reason for non-payment could well be the supplier's own fault, e.g. relevant supplier's staff were not informed that the wrong quality was delivered to a customer because of a poor communication system.

2 *Involving sales executives* in the credit control process. Remember that sales persons actually talk to customers at frequent intervals and may be able to provide valuable information.

3 *A penalty for introducing bad debts.* It is no use making a sale if you do not get paid. It would at least make sales people more careful about who they sell to. Sales could however fall, if sales people became over-cautious in accepting new business.

4 *Recognizing the customer's payment systems.* This would ensure that documentation such as invoices and statements arrive in time to obtain payment as early as practicable.

5 *Employing a debt collection specialist*, e.g. to collect debts from hire purchase debtors.
6 *Contra*. It may be possible to buy something on credit from your debtor and simply offset the debt.

Improvement in credit control can certainly enhance a firm's cash flow position within a relatively short space of time. This area of working capital management is dealt with more fully in Chapter 11.

Efficiency

Efficient use of fixed assets, improved inventory control, effective credit control and careful co-ordination of business functions can improve profitability and enable an even greater ploughback. It is therefore possible for a firm to produce more finance from internal sources simply by becoming more efficient in the ways it organizes, manages, operates and controls the scarce resources at its disposal. It should be noted that growth, e.g. in terms of turnover, and profitability do not always go hand in hand.

Retained profits

In the UK, one of the most important sources of capital is the retained (i.e. undistributed) profits. Companies must plough back profits in order to invest in new fixed assets, working capital, external investments and research and development, so as to secure their long-term progression and survival (see Figure 4.2). The net profit after tax and dividends may be in the form of the profit and loss account balance and/or general reserve; either way it has been ploughed back to self-finance company growth.

In the situation where the directors' dividend policy is to have a low dividend payout and a high ploughback, the ordinary shareholders should be compensated for this by the capital growth in the value of their shares. However, this does not always hold true, since there are many other variables which affect share prices.

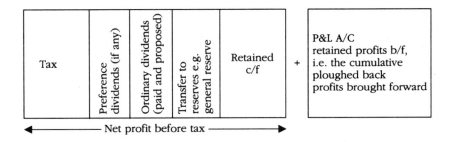

Figure 4.2 The appropriation of company profits

Finance from creditors

The time lag between the delivery of goods and the payment of suppliers provides short-term finance, e.g. 3 months. However, if discounts are offered in return for prompt payment, it could certainly be to the firm's advantage to pay promptly. The discount rate offered although small, could in fact have a substantial effective annual rate of interest in excess of 20 per cent. It must also be remembered that if firms place too much reliance upon finance from creditors this could cause their liquidity position to deteriorate.

Audit

The role of internal and external audit in the control and management of fixed assets and working capital should not be under-estimated. It is the responsibility of management to ensure that adequate systems of internal control are in operation. It is the task of the auditors to assess the efficiency of those systems and to inform management of any possible weaknesses. In this way losses due to errors and fraud may be minimized.

The banker's role: advising firms

Numerous reports and articles have over the years pointed to an 'information gap' as being responsible for firms having difficulty in obtaining finance from external sources. This obsession with the problems of raising funds from external sources, although very important, has in our view been at the expense of making firms more aware of their internal sources of capital. Firms not only need advice on how to obtain finance, they also need to know how to make the best possible use of it. It could well be the case, that nowadays there is such a wealth of information available that the real problem is a 'communication gap'. Thus, there is a great need for bankers to provide advice and communicate relevant information relating to both internal and external financing. Bankers are in a prime position to develop this ancillary advice service to meet the needs of their customers and to bridge the 'communication gap'. Banks have been instrumental in stimulating more interest in the use of budgetary control simply by requiring firms to produce cash flow forecasts in support of an application for an advance. Assistance given now to encourage firms to make better use of the finance they already employ can only prove to promote the banks' long-term success. If your banking customer can: (1) survive, (2) develop and grow, (3) become more efficient, and (4) manage more effectively, then the bank will also grow and prosper.

Conclusion

Management must strive to make better use of the funds they already possess. ROI (Return On Investment) is the real name of the game. An investment should yield an adequate return: for every investment has an opportunity cost. The productivity of capital and concern with cash flow are both areas of utmost importance. 'Buried treasure' can be found in the form of surplus assets, the type of replacement decision, more effective inventory control, more efficient credit control and by improving business efficiency. All of these may either increase cash flow and/or ensure more profits are available for retention. Bankers are in the front line when it comes to the provision of advice and communication of relevant business/financial information. Banks may, by helping firms improve their performance, secure their own long-term future. The banker as a business adviser can make a most worthwhile contribution to the recovery of British industry, in tomorrow's complex and diverse business environment.

SUMMARY

One of the principal and most important sources of finance is that which is 'self-generated' and ploughed back into the business. It is often referred to as 'retained earnings' or 'undistributed profits' and is represented in the reserves section of the balance sheet by the general reserve and profit-and-loss account balance and certain other revenue reserves.

Internal financing is concerned with:

- making better use of the finance which the company has already acquired, such as increasing the efficiency with which it is used, e.g. working capital management;
- releasing capital that is tied up in surplus fixed and current assets;
- ploughing back profits.

Self-assessments 4.1

(Review your attempted answers to these self-assessments with the appropriate section of this chapter.)

1   Explain why retained earnings is considered to be an important source of company finance.
2   What is meant by a 'strategy of surplus asset recognition and disposal', and what are its benefits?
3   How can a company become more efficient, as indicated in Figure 4.1 and therefore able to generate more finance internally?
4   In addition to the evaluation of the financial data, what other factors should be looked at when considering making an investment in a new fixed asset?
5   Explain ways in which management can improve:
    (a)   credit control; and
    (b)   inventory control.
6   Describe the ways in which a banker can help a small company manage its finances.

Note

1 Chadwick, L. (1980) 'Buried treasure', *Journal of the Institute of Bankers*, October.

Further reading

Back, R.D. (1977) 'The branch manager as an adviser to small firms', *Journal of the Institute of Bankers*, December.

Chadwick, L. (1977) 'The history of Holset Engineering 1952–1977', MBA Dissertation, University of Bradford.

Chadwick, L. (1980) 'Should we be more inward looking – for that extra finance', *Management Accounting*, February.

Muhlemann, A., Oakland, J. and Lockyer, K. (1992) *Production and Operations Management*, London: Pitman.

Woodward, H.N. (1976) 'Management strategies for small companies', *Certified Accountant*, August.

Chapter 5

Capital gearing

Objectives

When you have read this chapter you should be able to:

- understand that different companies have different capital structures;
- understand the difference between business risk and financial risk;
- define gearing;
- calculate gearing ratios, cover ratios and earnings per share;
- understand the effect that gearing can have on the earnings per share.

This chapter introduces you to the reasons why companies adopt different capital structures and the effects those structures can have on the earnings per share. Included in the chapter are a number of self-assessment questions.

CAPITAL STRUCTURE

The balance sheet equation of assets = capital plus liabilities indicates that the assets of a business are financed by a mixture of short-term, medium-term and long-term forms of capital. This chapter is concerned with the medium- and long-term sources.

A company may choose to use preference shares and/or loans (also known as debentures), as well as ordinary shares, to provide medium and long-term finance. The actual mix that the company adopts for its capital structure will depend on a number of factors but will probably include the degree of financial risk it wishes to take on board.

This will be influenced by the type of business it is engaged in, which will inevitably carry some business risk. If it has a high level of business risk, the directors may not wish to make the business even more precarious by incurring the additional financial risk associated with the issue of loan capital and preference shares. There is the danger that in poor trading periods it will be unable to meet its fixed-interest payments. If debentures are issued, interest has to be paid, whether profits are earned or not, whereas dividends on shares issued give some flexibility as they are somewhat discretionary. Therefore the ability to cope with adverse trading periods is an important factor for consideration.

The age and development of the company will also have to be considered. New firms are more risky than established businesses. They have no track record and therefore finance is less readily available. Another factor is the size of the company. Large companies have stability, strength and reputation and therefore there is more choice available to them. The above are an indication of the factors to be taken into consideration when deciding what form the capital structure will take.

Self-assessment 5.1

Distinguish between business risk and financial risk.

GEARING

Gearing (or financial leverage as it is sometimes called) is the relationship of equity funds (i.e. ordinary shares plus all the reserves) and loans/preference shares. It can be expressed by the following ratios:

$$\frac{\text{Long-term loans} + \text{Preference shares}}{\text{Equity}}$$

or

$$\frac{\text{Long-term loans} + \text{Preference shares}}{\text{Long-term loans} + \text{Preference shares} + \text{Equity}}$$

A company is said to be highly geared if the proportion of long-term loans and preference shares is high in relation to the equity funds, because the interest

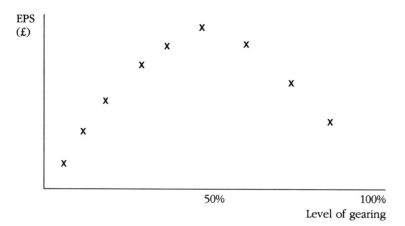

Figure 5.1   Gearing

payments and preference dividends could drastically reduce the pool available to the ordinary shareholders and the earnings per share falls. It can be depicted by Figure 5.1.

With the increased levels of gearing the ordinary shareholders benefit up to the point that the earnings per share starts to plateau and then fall. At this stage they have taken on board further risk without an increased return to compensate them. Consequently, the higher the gearing, the higher the risk to the ordinary shareholders. The stability of profits is therefore important. Why gear up you might ask? The answer is that the cost of loans and preference capital is cheaper than equity funds, as we shall see in Chapter 6 on the cost of capital.

Self-assessment 5.2

Define gearing.

The Black Manufacturing Co. Ltd has the following structure of finance:

	£000s
Ordinary shares of £1	2,700
Reserves	630
6% preference shares of £1	900
7% debentures (secured on the freehold premises)	1,620
Current liabilities	450
Total assets	6,300

The company's profits, before interest and corporation tax at 30 per cent amounted to £1.53 million. The ordinary dividend is usually 10p per share. The company is in a stable situation.

Is the company highly geared?

In order to answer this we need to calculate the above ratio, viz:

$$\frac{\text{Long-term loans} + \text{Preference shares}}{\text{Long-term loans} + \text{Preference shares} + \text{Equity}}$$

$$\frac{1{,}620 + 900}{2{,}700 + 630} = 75.7\%$$

This percentage is high and so the company appears to be highly geared.

How many times is the debenture interest covered?

To answer this question we need to prepare the profit and loss statement viz.:

	£000s
Profit before interest and taxation	1,530.00
Less: debenture interest (7% × 1,620)	113.40
	1,416.60
Less: corporation tax at 30%	424.98
	991.62
Less: preference dividend (6% × 900)	54.00
Available for the ordinary shareholders	937.62
Less: ordinary dividend (10% × 2,700)	270.00
Retained profits	667.62

The question can now be answered:

$$\frac{1,530.0}{113.4} = 13.5 \text{ times}$$

This indicates little likelihood of not being able to meet the interest payments, and leads us to conclude that perhaps the company is not, after all, highly geared.

What is the dividend cover for the preference and ordinary shares?

Preference dividend cover:

$$\frac{991.62}{54.0} = 18.4 \text{ times}$$

There also appears to be little likelihood of failing to meet this dividend payment.

Ordinary dividend cover:

$$\frac{937.62}{270.00} = 3.47 \text{ times}$$

The ordinary dividend is well covered. Both dividend cover ratios indicate that the company is not too highly geared.

Calculate the rate of return using (1) profit before interest and taxation: long-term finance, and (2) profit after preference dividend: equity.

(1) $\quad \dfrac{1,530}{2,700+630+900+1,620} = 26.15\%$

(2) $\quad \dfrac{937.62}{2,700+630} = 28.15\%$

Both appear to be reasonable returns.

Calculate the earnings per share (EPS).

$$\frac{937.62}{2,700} = 34.7p$$

If the company needed more capital, in what form would you recommend it be obtained?

The answer to this question appears to be long-term loans, but further analysis along the lines indicated above and noting the resultant effects is necessary before any conclusion can be drawn.

Self-assessment 5.3

The capital structures of three companies appear as follows:

	A Plc £000s	B Plc £000s	C Plc £000s
Ordinary shares (£1)	520	364	260
Reserves	250	250	250
7% preference shares	–	156	130
6% debentures	–	–	130

Each company made annual profits before interest, dividends and taxation (at 30%) of £104,000.

You are required: (1) to calculate the earnings per share for each of the three companies; (2) to state the conclusions you can draw.

Self-assessment 5.4

Billings Ltd has the following capital structure:

Ordinary shares of £1	£100,000
Reserves	50,000
6% debenture	40,000

Its profits before tax are reasonably stable around £20,000. Taxation is to be calculated at 30 per cent.

1   Is the company highly geared?
2   How many times is the debenture interest covered?
3   What is the ordinary dividend cover if the rate of dividend is usually 5 per cent?
4   What is the rate of return before tax on (a) equity and (b) total long-term finance?
5   Calculate the earnings per share.
6   If the company needed £50,000 additional long-term finance, in what form would you recommend it be obtained? Additional loans can be obtained at

6 per cent, and the £50,000 will generate the same average return as currently being achieved on all long-term finance. It is not expected that the dividend will be increased.

SUMMARY

The company must decide on its capital structure after carefully considering the effect that structure will have upon its earnings per share, cover ratios and return on capital, for if these suffer by gearing up, then the demand for the company's shares is likely to fall, and the shareholders' wealth will not have been maximized. Thus a fundamental objective of financial management will not have been achieved. Factors to be taken into account in coming to the decision include the level of business risk for the enterprise, the stability of profits, the taxation effects, and the financial returns (interest and dividends) demanded at different levels of risk. If these are carefully considered, then the capital structure adopted can lead to increased benefits for the ordinary shareholders.

Further reading

Pike, R. and Neale, B. (1993) *Corporate Finance and Investment*, London: Prentice Hall.
Weston, J.F. and Copeland, T.E. (1988) *Managerial Finance*, London: Cassell.

Chapter 6

The cost of capital

Objectives

When you have read this chapter you should be able to:

- identify the different component costs of capital;
- define each of the component costs discussed;
- calculate the weighted average cost of capital;
- understand how changes in the capital structure affect the weighted cost of capital.

This chapter introduces you to the concept that investors require compensation for risk by requiring a higher return and that different investments have different risks and returns. Included in the chapter are a number of self-assessment questions.

COMPONENT COSTS OF CAPITAL

There are variations in the costs of capital due to the fact that different kinds of investment carry different levels of risk which is compensated for by different levels of return on the investment. The cost of loan capital, also called debt capital, is the rate of interest payable on the loan. The cost of preference share capital is the rate of preference dividend, also called the coupon rate, divided by the net issue receipts, viz.:

$$\frac{\text{Rate of preference dividend}}{\text{Net issue receipts}} \quad \text{or} \quad \frac{Dp}{Pn}$$

For example, a firm issues 6 per cent preference shares for £100 par value and receives net proceeds of £95 after expenses. The cost of this capital is:

$$\frac{6}{95} \times 100 = 6.3\%$$

Adjustment for taxation

Tax on interest and dividends is treated differently. Interest is charged against profits, before the tax is calculated, whereas dividends are deducted from the after-tax profits. Therefore, investments made out of an issue of preference shares must yield a higher return than if loan capital was used.

Illustration

A company needs to raise £100,000 for a worthwhile project which is expected to yield 10 per cent. Its profit before obtaining the capital is £50,000.

	Before obtaining finance	*Yield on investment 10%*	*If debt is used @ 10%*	*If pref. capital used @ 10%*	*Required yield is 12%*
Profits	£50,000	£10,000	£60,000	£60,000	£62,000
Interest:					
10% × £100,000			10,000		
			50,000		
Tax @ say 50%	25,000		25,000	30,000	31,000
	25,000		25,000	30,000	31,000
Pref. dividend			–	10,000	6,000
Available for ordinary div.	25,000		25,000	20,000	25,000
				Insufficient to maintain current position	

Thus, if preference capital is used, the investment will have to yield 12 per cent, not the 10 per cent expected, otherwise the ordinary shareholder will be in a worse position than they are without the investment.

- *The cost of debt* can therefore be defined as the rate of return that must be earned on debt financed investments to keep unchanged the earnings available to the ordinary shareholders.
- *The cost of preference shares* is the rate of return that must be earned on preference share financed investments to keep unchanged the earnings available to the ordinary shareholders.
- *The cost of ordinary shares* and the reserves (i.e. equity) is the minimum rate of return that must be earned on equity financed investments to keep unchanged the value of the existing equity, i.e. if the cost of equity is 15 per cent, then only if the internal rate of return (for IRR refer to Chapter 8) exceeds 15 per cent on equity finance investments will the 15 per cent cost of capital be maintained. The rate of return is measured using the Gordon Shapiro model:

$$\frac{D}{P} + g \text{ being } \quad \frac{\text{Next dividend}}{\text{Share price}} + \text{Average growth in dividend (\%)}$$

- *The cost of retained earnings* is not zero, as you might expect. It is the same rate as equity. This is because as earnings are retained they go into the reserves, thus increasing equity.

- *The cost of a new issue of ordinary shares* is higher than for retained earnings, due to the expenses of issue.
- *The cost of depreciation funds* is the same as the weighted average cost of capital because a combined pool of finance will have been used to buy the assets on which the depreciation provision is based.

Self-assessment 6.1

From the following information calculate:

1   the cost of equity;
2   the cost of debt.

The expected growth in dividends	5%
The quoted share price	£4.35
The dividend per share	£0.87
The rate of tax	30%
9% loan stock	

WEIGHTED AVERAGE COST OF CAPITAL

The above individual component costs are brought together to form the weighted average cost of capital (WACC), where the 8 per cent loan stock has a market value of £45 million, the preference shares pay 10 per cent on a market value of £7 million and the equity has a market value of £98 million. The company pays a dividend of 33p per share, the growth in dividends is 5 per cent and the share price is £2.20. Tax at 40 per cent.

	(2) £m	(3) Gross	(4) Tax	(5) After tax	(6) (2) × (5)
Loan stock	45	8%	3.2%	4.8%	£2.16m
Pref. shares	7	10%		10.0%	£0.70m
Equity	98	20%*		20.0%	19.60m
	150				22.46m
WACC		$\frac{22.46}{150.00} = 14.97\%$			

$$* \frac{£0.33}{£2.20} + 5\% = 20\%$$

You will notice that the market values of the finance have been used rather than the book values shown in the balance sheet. This is to overcome the problem reflected by historic cost accounting. You should also note that the loan stock pays a lower return than is paid on the preference capital as it carries less risk to the investor, and the preference capital pays a lower return than the ordinary shareholders receive for the same reason. Thus the principle of the higher the risk the higher the required rate of return is recognized.

Self-assessment 6.2

From the following information calculate the weighted average cost of capital (WACC):

> 80,000 ordinary shares of £1 (market value £120,000)
> £40,000 6% loan stock quoted at £75 per £100 of stock
> Growth in dividend is 7%
> Expected dividend is 15p per share
> Reserves amount to £45,000
> Tax rate is 40%

Self-assessment 6.3

Calculate the new WACC if the company in 6.2 above raises a further £50,000 in loan stock at 9 per cent, this issue having only a second charge on the assets of the company. This issue would result in an increase in the expected dividend to 18p and leave the growth rate unaffected, but the added risk would cause the share price to fall to £1.25.

Self-assessment 6.4

Compare your solutions to 6.2 and 6.3. What conclusions can you draw?

Self-assessment 6.5

How will the ordinary share price be affected do you think if:

1 the 6% loan stock is redeemed;
2 future retained earnings have the effect of lowering the gearing level dramatically.

MARGINAL COST OF CAPITAL

The marginal cost of capital is the extra cost of obtaining an extra £1 of finance. If we refer to the information in 6.3 above and the solution later in the text we can calculate the marginal cost of capital (MCC) viz.:

> Marginal capital = £30,000
>
> Marginal cost = £2,844
>
> $\dfrac{2.844}{30} = 9.48\%$

The MCC might be more appropriate than the WACC for capital project evaluation.

SUMMARY

This chapter has been concerned with the nature of cost of capital. The various component costs have been defined and brought together in the calculation of the weighted average cost of capital, being a 'hurdle rate' which all project returns on investment must achieve. In this way the principle that the benefits must exceed their cost is satisfied. The cost of capital is central to the discussion of capital project appraisal in Chapter 8.

Further reading

Brealey, R. and Myers, S. (1991), *Principles of Corporate Finance*, London: McGraw Hill.
Weston, J.F. and Copeland, T.E. (1988), *Managerial Finance*, London: Cassell.

Chapter 7

Introduction to the theory of optimal gearing

Objectives

When you have read this chapter you should be able to:

- define gearing;
- identify three contrasting theories of the effects of gearing on the cost of capital;
- draw a graph, using data, depicting the traditional view;
- identify the capital asset pricing model;
- calculate the required rate of return for an investment using that model;
- understand the meaning of the term 'arbitrage'.

GEARING DEFINED

Gearing can be defined as the use of some funds which carry a fixed cost in the anticipation that the returns received from their use will exceed their cost. It is also expected that this excess will benefit the ordinary shareholders thus giving them a greater return overall. This is in accordance with the concept of maximization of shareholder wealth.

Traditional view

If we refer again to the chapter on the cost of capital we can see that the lowest component cost of capital relates to the fixed interest bearing investments. The cost of capital is thus interdependent upon the level of gearing. Therefore it could be argued that debt should be obtained up to the level, at which the company's average cost of capital is at its lowest (see Figure 7.1).

With the increase in risk, both debt and equity investors require higher returns, which forces the average cost of capital to rise. The optimal level is where the average cost of capital is at its lowest. Up to that point the company should minimize its cost of capital and thus increase its market value per share. After a certain level of risk has been reached any further increase in debt increases the risk to the ordinary shareholders. They would then require a higher

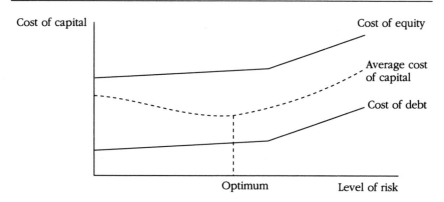

Figure 7.1 Traditional view
Source: J. C. Van Horne

return, i.e. a risk premium. The risk premium could be determined using the capital asset pricing model:

$$Rj = i + (\bar{R}m - i)\, Bj \quad \text{where} \quad Rj = \text{expected return on the investment } j$$

$$i = \text{interest-free rate}$$

$$\bar{R}m = \text{average market return}$$

$$Bj = \text{Beta for the investment } j$$

Source: W.F. Sharpe

Illustration

Risk free rate is 10%
Average market return is 16%
Beta is 1.00, but with increased gearing it becomes 1.25

At present $Rj = 0.10 + (0.16 - 0.10)\, 1.00 = 16\%$

After gearing $Rj = 0.10 + (0.16 - 0.10)\, 1.25 = 17.5\%$

that is, the expected return for the investment increases from 16% to 17.5% as the Beta (the measure of risk) increases from 1.00 to 1.25. The risk premium in this case is 1.5% (i.e. 17.5 − 16.0).

Self-assessment 7.1

Using the capital asset pricing model and the following data, calculate the required rate of return for the investment:

Risk free rate	4%
Average return on the Market Portfolio	12%
Beta coefficient	1.25

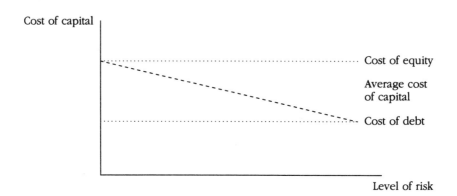

Figure 7.2   Hypothetical view
Source: D. Durand

Hypothetical view

This was advocated by Durand in 1952 as the net income approach, whereby the cost of capital could be reduced by the greater use of debt (see Figure 7.2).

The hypothetical view assumes that the ordinary shareholders will not require a higher return with increased levels of gearing caused by the use of increasing levels of debt. A further assumption is that the lenders themselves will not require higher returns with the increasing levels of debt. Consequently, there is no upturn in the cost of either equity or debt and the average cost of capital falls until the level of debt is reached.

Modigliani Miller view

This view, first put forward in 1958 and amended for taxation in 1963, states that the cost of capital is independent of the capital structure and therefore there is no optimal level (see Figure 7.3).

The cost of equity will rise by an amount just sufficient to offset any possible saving or loss. The supply of debt is determined by the lenders. Modigliani Miller (MM) believe that the optimal level is simply the maximum amount of debt which lenders are prepared to subscribe in any given circumstances, e.g. level of inflation, rate of economic growth, level of profits etc. They argue that investors will exercise their own leverage by mixing their own portfolio with debt and shares. They call this the 'arbitrage process'. Under these circumstances the cost of capital is constant. There has been a great deal of empirical work carried out since their view was first expressed, which has added to the debate.

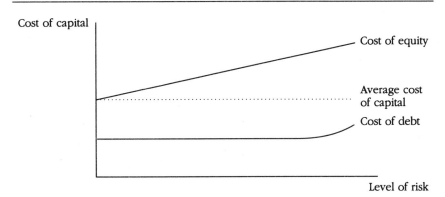

Figure 7.3   Modigliani Miller View

Illustration

Companies A and B are identical except that A is ungeared and B is geared:

	A	B
Value of equity	£500,000	£375,000
Value of debt	—	250,000
	500,000	625,000

The following information is also applicable:

	A	B
Yield on equity	20%	20%
Yield on debt		10%
Profit before interest	£100,000	£100,000
Interest on debt		£25,000

From this we are able to calculate the WACC for each company:

		A	B
	100% × 20% =	20%	
$\frac{375}{625}$ = 60% × 20% =			12%
$\frac{250}{625}$ = 40% × 10% =			4%
			16%

Note, that with the introduction of gearing into its capital structure, B is able to reduce its WACC from 20 per cent to 16 per cent.

Let us now calculate the amount of profit available to the ordinary shareholders. We shall ignore taxation.

	A	B
Profit before interest	£100,000	£100,000
Less: interest	—	25,000
	£100,000	75,000

If Mr Troy, an investor in B, holds 1,000 shares, what is the amount of his income?

$$\frac{1,000}{375,000} \times £75,000 = £200 \text{ income}$$

If Mr Troy decides to sell his holding in B and equate the same gearing level in his own portfolio by borrowing funds at the rate of 10 per cent, what will be the amount he needs to borrow?

The gearing level in B is $250/375 = 2/3$rds.

Therefore $2/3 \times 1,000 = 667$
i.e.
He sells   1,000 shares for cash
He borrows $\dfrac{667}{1,667}$

Note: $667/1,667 = 40\%$ the same as $250/625$

What will Mr Troy's total income be, if he invests the total funds available in A?

$$\frac{1,667}{500,000} \times 100,000 = £333 \text{ from shares}$$

Less, borrowed:

$$10\% \times 667 = \frac{£67}{£266} \text{ interest payable}$$

As his income has increased by £66 for the same level of risk, Mr Troy would be well advised to implement the above sale, borrow and purchase. The above is an illustration of the arbitrage process described by Modigliani Miller.

The question arises as to whether B is fairly valued. In fact it appears to be overvalued by the stock market. With the same company/personal gearing level the returns should be the same. Also only £200 income is receivable instead of £266. If investors at large follow Mr Troy's action, there will be reduced demand for the shares in B thus forcing down their share price. On the other hand the extra demand for the shares in A will force their share price up. This process will continue until the total value of A is equal to the total value of B, i.e. at £600,000. Once this has occurred there will be no advantage to another investor of 1,000 shares in B repeating the action of Mr Troy.

Self-assessment 7.2

Honley Plc and Garforth Plc are both public companies whose shares are quoted on the Stock Exchange. Both generate profits before charging debenture interest, of £2 million, and it is expected that they will continue to do so for the foreseeable future. Both companies are considered to be subject to identical business risk. Honley is financed entirely by 3 million ordinary shares, which have a market value of £2.50 each ex. dividend. Garforth Plc has issued £2 million undated 6 per cent debenture stock which has a current market yield of 8 per cent. The ordinary share capital of Garforth Plc comprises 1,762,500 ordinary shares whose market value is £3.20 each ex. dividend.

It is the policy of both companies to distribute all available profits as dividends at the end of each year.

You are required to:

1 Calculate the cost of equity and the weighted average cost of capital for each company, based on market values. Tax to be taken at 25 per cent.
2 Explain the reasons for any difference between:
    (a) the cost of equity for each company; and
    (b) the WACC for each company as revealed in (1) above.
3 Calculate the yield on equity after tax for each company and the yield on debt for Garforth Plc before tax.
4 What is the amount of income of Mr Lister, an investor in Garforth, if he holds 2,000 shares.
5 If Mr Lister decides to sell his holding in Garforth Plc, and equate the same gearing level in his own portfolio by borrowing funds at the rate of 10 per cent, what will be the amount he needs to borrow?
6 If he invests the total funds available in Honley, what will his income be?
7 What is the term used to describe the above action taken by Mr Lister?

Self-assessment 7.3

Queensgate Plc has produced the following table for different levels of gearing:

% level of debt	% cost of debt (after tax)	% WACC
0	8	18
10	8	17
20	9	16.2
30	10	17
40	12	18
50	14	19
60	17	21
70	25	28

You are required:

1 To calculate the percentage cost of equity for each of the levels of debt. Hint: $(0\% \times 8) + (100\% \times Ke) = $ WACC of 18% $\therefore Ke = 18\%$

2 To prepare a graph indicating the cost of debt, the cost of equity and the weighted average cost of capital (WACC).

3 To indicate the effects of the different levels of debt and the theory represented in (2).

4 To state the percentage level of debt at which the optimal level of gearing is indicated.

5 To calculate the Beta coefficient for the cost of equity calculated in (1) above at the 70 per cent level of gearing, if the risk free rate is 5 per cent and the expected return on the market portfolio is 18 per cent. The beta for a company with zero gearing in the sector of industry in which Queensgate Plc operates is estimated to be 1.0. What conclusions do you draw?

Self-assessment 7.4

Make a list of items to show that you understand the significance of gearing to the financial manager.

SUMMARY

Two contrasting views have been expressed. Firstly, managers should take on debt to the point where the cost of capital is minimized. This might be a range rather than a specific point. Secondly, MM suggest that either debt or equity should be used rather than attempting to obtain any advantage from the mixing of debt with equity as the average cost of capital will not be affected by the mixture.

However, the higher the level of debt the greater the risk, which can have an effect on both profitability and liquidity. This could lead to the imposition of external constraints being imposed, for instance, the appointment of a receiver. The overall objective must still be to maximize the value of the firm for the long-run benefit of the ordinary shareholders.

Further reading

Brealey, R. and Myers, S. (1991) *Principles of Corporate Finance*, London: McGraw Hill.

Durand, D. (1959) 'The cost of debt and equity funds for business', in E. Solomon (ed.) *Management of Corporate Capital*, New York: Free Press, 91–116.

Modigliani, F. and Miller, M.H. (1958) 'The cost of capital, corporate finance and the theory of investment', *American Economic Review*, June, 48: 261–97.

Sharpe, W.F. (1964) 'Capital asset prices: a theory of market equilibrium under conditions of risk', *Journal of Finance*, September, 19: 425–42.

Van Horne, J.C. (1994) *Financial Management and Policy*, US: Prentice Hall.

Weston, J.F. and Copeland, T.E. (1988) *Managerial Finance*, London: Cassell.

Section III

Investing the finance

Chapter 8

Capital investment appraisal

Objectives

When you have read this chapter you should be able to:

- identify the methods commonly used in the assessment of capital investment projects;
- understand the concept of the time value of money;
- recognize worthwhile projects based upon the decision rules associated with discounted cash flow methods.

THE CAPITAL INVESTMENT DECISION

The capital investment decision is long-term in nature and is otherwise known as capital budgeting. Such decisions affect all future accounting periods until the project has expired. Examples include the purchase of new plant and machinery, the addition of a new product line or the closing down of an existing factory. Because different projects last for different lengths of time, the time value of money comes into consideration. The time value of money can be expressed in the following way. If you were offered £100 today or £100 in a month's time, which option would you prefer. You will no doubt go for the option of £100 today. In doing so you have recognized the time value of money, as £1 today is worth more than £1 receivable at some future date, even ignoring inflation.

Capital budgeting involves the making of long-term decisions for investment projects, whose benefits will be realized at some future date and also the provision of the necessary finance to carry out the proposal. Because the future is hard to predict, due to risk and uncertainty, decisions in this area are amongst the most difficult to make.

In order to make a rational decision we require a hurdle rate against which the project's rate of return is measured. The amount of the return must be measured against the level of investment required. If you were offered a return of £25 at the end of one year on your investment, you would need to measure that amount against the level of investment required. The amount of £25 is meaningless on its own. If you were asked to invest £100 you would be able to calculate the rate of return as 25 per cent p.a. This is good return when compared with alternative opportunities. But if you were required to invest £1,000, a return of 2.5 per cent is not very good. You therefore need to know both the level of investment required and the amount of the return over the future time periods. Of course you would also expect that the higher the return the higher the risk, so the relative riskiness of the project would also need to be assessed.

Capital projects do not just appear on their own. They need to be generated through programmes of research and development. Choice must then be exercised between the projects available, ranking them in order of acceptability. Mutually exclusive projects must be identified and the independent items within the project must be known. Good data is therefore of paramount importance.

METHODS USED IN THE ASSESSMENT OF THE PROJECTS

The methods of assessment fall under two main headings viz.: surplus and non-surplus methods. The non-surplus methods are based on status, internal politics and social need, such as pollution control. In this text we are concerned with the surplus methods, viz.: accounting rate of return, payback and discounted cash flow.

Accounting rate of return

Illustration

A project is expected to have an initial cost at the start of year 1 of £32,000 and to yield the following cash flows at the end of:

Year 1	£8,000
Year 2	£20,000
Year 3	£14,000
Year 4	£6,000
	£48,000

The average cash inflow is	48,000/4	=	£12,000
The depreciation per annum is	32,000/4	=	£ 8,000
The average accounting profit is	12,000–8,000	=	£ 4,000
The average capital employed is	32,000/2	=	£16,000
The accounting rate of return is	4,000/16,000	=	25%

Self-assessment 8.1

A project is expected to have an initial cost at the start of year 1 of £30,000 and yield the following cash flows at the end of:

Year 1	£9,000
Year 2	£12,000
Year 3	£10,000
Year 4	£9,000
Year 5	£5,000

You are required to calculate the accounting rate of return.

Payback

Payback is the length of time it takes for the project to recover the capital cost of the investment. It incorporates profit and time as well as cost. One of its weaknesses, unless discounting techniques are used, is that it does not take account of the time value of money. Non-discounted payback is called traditional payback.

Illustration

Year 0 (i.e. the start of year 1)		
	Cash outflow	£32,000
Year 1 (i.e. the end of year 1)		
	Cash inflows	£8,000
Year 2		£20,000
Year 3		£14,000
Year 4		£6,000

By the end of year 2 the project has paid back £28,000 and by the end of year 3, £42,000. It therefore pays back between the second and third years. The exact timing is as follows:

2 years + (4,000/14,000) × 365 = 2 years and 104 days

where £4,000 of the £14,000 is needed to take the £28,000 to £32,000.

This project would be accepted if this payback period was within the acceptable time period laid down by management or it was less than the payback period of an alternative project under consideration.

Traditional payback ignores cash flows received after the initial investment has been paid back. It can be used by management looking for returns over the short term or those not planning too far ahead. Risk increases as projections are made into the future, so the use of payback can be useful in the reduction of risk. On the other hand, some projects may take a long time before they become operational and yield returns. By using traditional payback these projects may be regarded by management as unsuitable and not given the consideration they deserve. Such projects might be fundamental to the long-term development of the firm, particularly if a change in direction is called for.

Self-assessment 8.2

Using the data in 8.1, calculate the traditional payback.
The limitations of payback can be summarised as follows:

1   It ignores the fact that some returns are received after the payback period
    and also the time value of money, i.e. £1 received today is more valuable
    than £1 received tomorrow.
2   Long-range plans are often shelved.
3   It fails to take into account the interest factor.

The principles of discounting

Using a rate of 10 per cent, £100 will accumulate to £110 by the end of year 1
and £121 by the end of year 2 using compound interest, thus:

	Now		Year 1		Year 2
Compounding	100	$\longrightarrow$	110	$\longrightarrow$	121

By discounting, the cash received in years 1 and 2 are converted into present
values, thus:

Discounting   100 $\longleftarrow$ 110

                   100 $\longleftarrow$ 121

Present value factors:

$$\frac{100}{110} \longleftarrow £1$$

$$= 0.909$$

being $\dfrac{100}{(1+10)^1}$

$$\frac{100}{121} \longleftarrow £1$$

$$= 0.826$$

being $\dfrac{100}{(1+10)^2}$

which can be expressed by the formula $P = \dfrac{S}{(1+r)^n}$

Where P = the value in present value terms
      S = the amount received at some future date
      r = the discount rate
      n = the number of years to the future date

It is not necessary to work out the discount factors as these are usually
provided. Refer to Appendix 3 at the back of this book.

Discounted payback

Here the cash flows are discounted before the payback period is worked out.

Illustration

A project is expected to have an initial cost at the start of year 1 of £32,000 and to yield the following cash flows at the end of:

Year 1	£ 8,000
Year 2	£20,000
Year 3	£14,000
Year 4	£ 6,000

The cost of capital is estimated to be 10%. The discounted payback period is calculated:

			Discounted cash flow (DCF)	*Cumulative*
Year 1	8,000	0.909	7,272	7,272
Year 2	20,000	0.826	16,520	23,792
Year 3	14,000	0.751	10,514	34,306
Year 4	6,000	0.683	4,098	38,404

It can be seen that the initial cost is paid back during year 3. Specifically:
2 years + 8,208/10,514 × 365 = 2 years 285 days

Self-assessment 8.3

What would the discounted payback period be if the discount rate was 15 per cent?

Net present value

Discounting the cash flow incorporates the opportunity cost of capital, which reflects the time value of money. The net present value can be defined as the present value of future net returns, discounted at the cost of capital, less the initial cost of the investment.

Illustration

A project is expected to have an initial cost at the start of year 1 of £32,000 and to yield the following cash flows at the end of:

Year 1	£ 8,000
Year 2	£20,000
Year 3	£14,000
Year 4	£ 6,000

The cost of capital is estimated to be 10 per cent.
The net present value is calculated as follows:

			Discounted cash flow (DCF)
Year 1	8,000	0.909	7,272
Year 2	20,000	0.826	16,520
Year 3	14,000	0.751	10,514
Year 4	6,000	0.683	4,098
			38,404
Less: initial cost			32,000
Net present value (NPV)			6,404

As the NPV is positive, i.e. the discounted net cash flows exceed the initial cost, the project is acceptable. This is based on the following assumptions:

1 The amounts and timing of the cash inflows and outflows are correctly forecast.
2 The opportunity cost of capital is correct.
3 There are no non-financial considerations which would make the project unacceptable.

Self-assessment 8.4

Calculate the NPV for the data contained in Self-assessment 8.3.

Internal rate of return

The internal rate of return can be defined as the rate of interest which equates the present value of future returns to the initial cost, i.e. where the NPV is zero.

Illustration

A project is expected to cost £15,000 and will have net cash inflows of £2,000, £8,000, £6,000 and £2,000 at the end of each of the next 4 years.

	NCF	Discount factor		Discounted cash flows	
		7%	8%	7%	8%
Yr 1	2,000	0.935	0.926	1,870	1,852
2	8,000	0.873	0.857	6,984	6,856
3	6,000	0.816	0.794	4,896	4,764
4	2,000	0.763	0.735	1,526	1,470
				15,276	14,942

The £15,000 falls between the two cash flows, therefore the IRR is between 7 per cent and 8 per cent. By interpolation the exact IRR is found:

Total range   = 15,276 − 14,942 = 334
Excess over cost = 15,276 − 15,000 = 276
7% + 276/334   = 7.826%

If the cost of capital is less than the IRR the project should be accepted. It should be noted that accuracy is lost if interpolation is carried out over more than a discount rate range of 1 per cent. In this case it is necessary to make the following amendment to the calculation. If the cost was between say 15 per cent and 20 per cent (rather than 7 per cent and 8 per cent) then the calculation would be:

15% + ((Excess over cost/Total range) × 20 − 15)

Self-assessment 8.5

A project is expected to cost £35,000 and have net cash inflows over the next 3 years of £15,000, £20,000 and £7,000.

1 Calculate the IRR for the project.
2 Using a cost of capital of 10 per cent calculate the NPV.
3 State whether the project is worthwhile.

SUMMARY

This chapter has considered the methods commonly used in the assessment of capital projects. The non-discounted methods of accounting rate of return and traditional payback have been compared with the discounted methods of discounted payback, net present value and internal rate of return. The discounted methods are considered to be superior as they take into account the time value of money, expressed as an opportunity cost of capital in the form of a discount rate. The overall objective of maximizing the value of the firm is reflected in the net present value method.

Further reading

Brealey, R. and Myers, S. (1991) *Principles of Corporate Finance*, London: McGraw Hill.
Weston, J.F. and Copeland, T.E. (1988) *Managerial Finance*, London: Cassell.

Chapter 9

Introduction to risk in capital budgeting

Objectives

When you have read this chapter you should be able to:

- name four methods of handling risk in capital budgeting;
- make calculations to take account of risk;
- identify worthwhile projects after adjusting for risk.

INTRODUCTION

So far we have assumed certainty in the cash flows. However, this will not be the case in a real-world situation. We therefore need to take into account risk, which can be defined as the likely variability of returns receivable from the project. Capital budgeting involves the estimation of the cost of the project, the net cash flows that will accrue if the project is undertaken, and the cost of capital used for discounting. If two projects are not equally risky, then this fact ought to be recognized before the final selection is made.

KINDS OF RISK

There is a risk attached to errors in estimating:

1 the cost and timing of the payments relating to the project;
2 the demand for the product and the selling price obtainable;
3 the production costs involved;
4 the life of the project;
5 the amount of working capital required.

There is also a risk caused by changes in the environment:

1 government restructuring of the taxation system, whereby the capital allowances (depreciation allowed for tax purposes) are altered;
2 government and local government legislation, such as building regulations or pollution controls;
3 scarcity of production resources.

APPROACHES TO HANDLING RISK

Several approaches have been developed to handle risk which include risk premium, coefficient of variation, probability, and the capital asset pricing model.

Risk premium

Some firms, having determined their basic rate of return add on a percentage to cover risk. This percentage is called a risk premium, e.g. basic rate of return of 14 per cent. If the project is considered to be low-risk then a premium of (say) 6 per cent would be added. If the project is considered to be quite risky, then a premium of (say) 15 per cent would be added. The higher the risk, the higher the premium. The cash flows would then be discounted at 20 per cent and 29 per cent respectively. A project that does not satisfy the normal decision rules for NPV or IRR would be rejected. It can be seen that the level of premium selected is subjective. However, the use of the capital asset pricing model may overcome this subjectivity by providing the required rate of return for the level of risk involved.

Self-assessment 9.1

What will be the effect on the NPV of increasing the discount rate by adding a risk premium?

Coefficient of variation

The coefficient of variation is a measure of relative dispersion and is calculated by dividing the standard deviation of the cash flows of the project by the mean (average) of the cash flows.

Illustration

Project X has a standard deviation (SD) of £300 and a mean of £1,000.
  The coefficient of variation is 300/1,000 = 0.3

Self-assessment 9.2

What is the coefficient of variation for project Y which has a SD of £300 and a mean of £4,000?

  It can be seen that project X has a higher coefficient of variation than project Y and therefore is more risky due to the effects of variation. This method of evaluation is used where £s returned are used rather than a percentage rate of return.

It should also be recognized that the standard deviation on its own is a weaker method than the coefficient of variation. In this case both projects had the same standard deviation which by that method of assessment alone would suggest that both projects were of equal risk. The coefficient of variation method shows that this is not the case.

Probability

This involves multiplying subjective probabilities by the possible discounted cash flows. The sum of the outcomes is called the expected value. The sum of the probabilities must always equal 1.

Illustration

	Project A		
Probability	*DCF*		
0.10	£3,000	=	300
0.20	3,500	=	700
0.40	4,000	=	1,600
0.20	4,500	=	900
0.10	5,000	=	500
	Expected value		£4,000

There is a 10 per cent chance that the discounted cash flows will be £3,000, a 20 per cent chance that they will be £3,500 etc.

Self-assessment 9.3

Calculate the expected value for project B, given the following probable outcomes:

10% – £2,000, 20% – £3,000, 40% – £3,500, 20% – £5,500, 10% – £6,000.

Project A with the higher expected value is the preferred, risk-adjusted, project.

Self-assessment 9.4

You are the financial manager of Green Ltd, a bottling company. You are trying to choose between two types of new equipment – brand EM and brand Super EM. The proposals have the following discrete profitability distributions of cash flow in each of the next 4 years:

Proposal EM		Proposal Super EM	
Probability	Net cash inflow	Probability	Net cash inflow
0.10	£3,000	0.10	£1,000
0.25	4,000	0.25	2,000
0.30	5,000	0.30	3,000
0.25	6,000	0.25	4,000
0.10	7,000	0.10	5,000

Required

1 For each proposal compute:
   (a) the expected value of the cash inflows in each of the next 4 years;
   (b) the coefficient of variation, given that the standard deviation for each project is, by coincidence, £1,140.
2 Which proposal has the greater degree of risk? (Give reasons.)

Capital asset pricing model

The capital asset pricing model (CAPM) is shown below:

$$RRR = Rf + (Rm - Rf)\,B$$

where RRR = the required rate of return
Rf = the risk-free rate
Rm = the average return on the market portfolio
B = the Beta coefficient which measures the volatility of risk

A Beta of 1.0 indicates the same risk as that of the market, whereas higher than 1.0 indicates that the project is more risky. The risk premium is reflected by the difference between the unadjusted discount rate and the required rate of return calculated from the model.

Illustration

Calculate the required rate of return given the following information. The risk-free rate in the economy is 10 per cent. The expected return on a market portfolio of investments is 15 per cent. The measure of the volatility of risk, i.e. the Beta coefficient is estimated to be 1.6.

$$RRR = 0.10 + (0.15 - 0.10) \times 1.6$$
$$= 0.10 + 0.08$$
$$= 18\%$$

Self-assessment 9.5

A company is considering investing in a risky new project. The following data has been ascertained:

Risk-free rate	3%
Return on market portfolio	12%
Beta coefficient	1.3

Calculate the required rate of return and state whether the project should be undertaken if the expected return is 18 per cent.

SUMMARY

In this chapter, four different methods of handling risk in capital budgeting have been considered. It should be pointed out that there are others which will be encountered in more advanced studies. The simplest method of handling risk is to increase the discount rate by a risk premium. The capital asset pricing model indicates the discount rate to be used, including the risk premium. Two statistical methods have been used, viz.: probability and coefficient of variation. Reference has also been made to the weakness of using the standard deviation in isolation.

Further reading

Brealey, R. and Myers, S. (1991) *Principles of Corporate Finance*, London: McGraw Hill.
Dixon, R. (1994) *Investment Appraisal*, London: CIMA/Kogan Page.
Lumby, S. (1994) *Investment Appraisal*, London: Chapman and Hall.
Weston, J.F. and Copeland, T.E. (1988) *Managerial Finance*, London: Cassell.

Chapter 10

Leases and leasing

Objectives

- On completion of this chapter you should be able to:
- distinguish between 'a finance lease' and 'an operating lease';
- appreciate the advantages claimed as to why companies/organizations may prefer to lease certain fixed assets, and their drawbacks;
- point out some of the terms in a lease concerned with land and buildings which the lessee should take particular note of;
- prepare a computation of taxation capital allowances using a 25 per cent writing-down allowance;
- calculate using present value tables, and taking tax into account whether the purchase of a fixed asset outright is better or worse than leasing the fixed asset;
- appreciate that the computations prepared are not the 'be all and end all' of decision making.

The CIMA, management accounting official terminology defines a lease as:

A contract between a lessor and a lessee for the hire of a specific asset.

The lessor retains ownership of the asset but conveys the right to the use of the asset to the lessee for an agreed period for the payment of specified rentals (SSAP 21).

The principal difference between the two types of lease shown in Figure 10.1 is concerned with which of the two parties, lessor or lessee is responsible

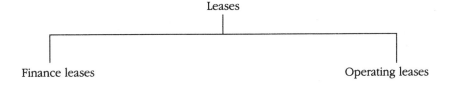

Figure 10.1 Types of lease

for most of the risk. In their official terminology, CIMA define a finance lease as:

A lease that transfers substantially all the risks and rewards of ownership of an asset to the lessee. A finance lease may also be called a 'capital lease' or a 'full pay-out lease'.

and an operating lease, on the other hand, is defined as:

A lease other than a finance lease. The lessor retains most of the risk and rewards of ownership. An operating lease may also be called a 'part-pay-out lease'.

To be classed as a finance lease it is presumed that a transfer of the risks and rewards take place if at the outset of the lease the present value of the minimum lease payments, including any initial payment, amounts to substantially all (normally 90 per cent or more) of the fair value of the leased asset (*in this context 'fair value' refers to the price at which the asset could be exchanged in an arm's length transaction less any grants received*). The present value would be calculated using the interest rate implicit in the lease.

The lessee in a finance lease will be responsible for repairs, maintenance and insurance. The lessor in such a lease plays a purely financial role. When a lease comes to an end it may be possible for the lessee to negotiate a secondary lease, possibly at a much reduced rental. This could well be the case where the lessor had recovered their outlay and expected profit. However, it may be possible when a lease comes to an end that ownership may pass to the lessee.

Leasing relates to the way in which a fixed asset is financed and as such is unaffected by the economic or operating risks of each particular project.

WHY LEASE?

Leasing does claim to have a number of advantages which are attractive enough to encourage companies/organizations to lease certain fixed assets. The advantages claimed include:

- To be able to acquire a fixed asset without having to pay for it outright around the date of acquisition, i.e. *there is no need to find a lump sum.*
- To, in effect, make the fixed assets/project which uses the fixed assets *self-financing.* As the asset/project generates cash flow the lease payments can, hopefully, be met as and when they become due. It can be described as an aid to cash flow management and a way in which a company/organization's liquidity can be improved.
- Providing a *hedge against obsolescence.* If machinery, plant or equipment is purchased outright and at some future date becomes obsolete because of changes in technology or some other reason, the company/organization has

to stand the loss incurred. The leasing of such fixed assets, tends to be for short periods of time, e.g. 3 years, 5 years. This means that the lessee can keep up with changes in technology because the leases come to an end at frequent intervals. As and when necessary, when leases do end, a replacement can be leased which is more appropriate to the needs of the company/organization. Even if the company/organization had to breach a lease agreement because the asset was obsolete, the penalty paid could be much less than the loss which could have been incurred, had the asset concerned been purchased outright.

- Unlike a loan or bank overdraft, the funding provided via a *lease cannot be withdrawn* unless the terms of the lease are broken, e.g. failure to insure the asset or to keep it in a good state of repair, or by the mutual agreement of both parties.

- The rates of interest on loans may be fixed or fluctuating, practice tends to favour fluctuating rates of interest. The *rate of interest* specified in the lease agreement will tend to be fixed and therefore constant. Whether or not this is an advantage all depends upon what happens to interest rates. It does however, mean that for a specified period of time there will be a similar amount being paid out as each payment becomes due which can be a help in providing stability and making cash flow planning much easier.

- *Tax reasons*. Governments come and go and so do taxation capital allowances and the rates of tax. In the leasing situation, the lessor claims whatever capital allowances are available and may pass on some of the benefit via lower leasing charges to the lessee. The amount, if any, which is passed on will depend upon competition within the market and also on how close the lease is to the lessor's year end. If it is possible for a lessor to do business in the period which is just before its year end, it may, because of the tax advantages, e.g. earlier relief, be prepared to offer the lessee a special deal!

  From the lessee's point of view the payments made under the lease in the UK are classed as charges which can be deducted in computing taxable income. However, the same rules apply to loan interest and hire purchase interest, i.e. they are also allowed as deductions in computing taxable profits in the UK. The tax position needs to be carefully monitored, as it changes from time to time, and this can have a significant impact on the lease versus loan decision.

- *Security* and/or a *satisfactory financial performance record*, i.e. 'a track record' may be needed to obtain a loan. It is not a prerequisite for obtaining a lease. Thus, a company with lots of growth but short of cash which could be described as 'a problem child' (see the amended Boston Matrix, Chapter 3), could find leasing quite attractive, e.g. for cash flow reasons and because of restricted access to other sources of finance caused by a lack of security, or its performance record to date.

- Clauses in certain leasing agreements may be *restrictive*, e.g. a restriction on the amount of debt financing via a maximum gearing ratio. This does have the disadvantage of constraining the company's activities, 'a lease with strings attached', but it does have the advantage of forcing the company not to become too highly geared which could prove dangerous if trading conditions deteriorate.
- It may be possible to raise finance via a '*sale and leaseback.*' For example, a local authority sells a building to an insurance company and then leases the building back. This provides the local authority with a lump sum with which to finance other projects. The local authority would, however, lose the right to any future capital gains (or losses)!

LEASING PLANT, MACHINERY AND EQUIPMENT

The amounts which companies expend on this area does have to be reported in their published accounts. The terms can be varied, but for those finance leases tend to require the lessee to insure the assets, clean it, repair it and maintain it. A lot of what you study within financial management tends to look at leases associated with these types of assets.

LEASING LAND AND BUILDINGS

Leases can be described as: long, over 50 years; or short, under 50 years. Here is an example of some of the items which could be included in a lease relating to land and buildings.

- *The term.* The lease is granted for a term of 20 years commencing on 11 June 19X3.
- *The lump sum payable.* On signing, the purchaser (the lessee) shall pay the vendor (the lessor) £250,000.
- *The rent.* The rent will be £36,000 per annum payable quarterly, in advance on 1 January, 1 April, 1 July and 1 October.
- *Rent review.* The rent is subject to review on 11 June 19X8 and every five years thereafter. In the event of failing to agree a new rental, the matter may be decided by an independent surveyor appointed by the Royal Institution of Chartered Surveyors.
- *Option to purchase.* The tenant (lessee); on giving 3 months' notice has the option to purchase the property at a figure to be agreed with the lessor.
- *Lessees' responsibilities.* The lessee is responsible for all internal and external repairs and decorations. The landlords insure the building and the costs of insurance are fully recoverable by the landlord.

The lease then goes on to place restrictions on the use of the building and warns of the landlord's right to repossess in the event of default, e.g. non-payment of rent, or failure to meet the responsibilities detailed in the lease.

Points to note for this type of lease are, that a lump sum would be paid out at the outset, that rent is payable in advance and also subject to a 5-yearly review. Also note, that the option to purchase could only go ahead if an agreement could be reached between the two parties on price and that the lessee can be responsible for a whole host of repairs, and finally the restrictions relating to the use of the building.

Leasing of buildings may provide some flexibility, e.g. the ability to move to other premises at some future date without having to sell the building. However, the terms may be such, as illustrated above, that they do have significant cash flow implications and future risks, e.g. higher rents which are also paid in advance.

THE LEASE VERSUS BUY DECISION

There are a number of ways in which to evaluate and compare the leasing or buying of plant, machinery, equipment and other fixed assets such as motor vehicles. One way of comparing the two, is as follows.

Buying

Taking into account the initial cost, residual value (if any), taxation capital allowances, and using the after tax cost of borrowing as the discount rate.

Leasing

Discounting the lease payments using the after tax cost of borrowing as the discount rate and taking account of any rebate, e.g. a percentage of the salvage value which accrues to the lessee.

The following example will provide you with an insight into the calculation side of generating comparative information: Pamfleur Plc are considering either purchasing or leasing a new piece of semi-automatic equipment.

Buying	Outright cost £400,000	Residual value £96,000 in 5 years' time
Leasing for 5 years	Cost £100,000 per year	Residual value £60,000 returned to lessee in 5 years' time

The aftertax cost of debt is 8%

Taxation assumptions

Capital allowances at the rate of 25% per annum on a reducing balance basis.

The rate of corporation tax: 33%

There will be a 1-year time lag between claiming the allowances and receiving the benefit, the first year to benefit will be year 2. The company does pay tax and can offset the tax relief.

Buying

First of all, we work out the tax benefit, via a capital allowances computation.

Year	Cost or written down value b/f	Writing down allowance at 25%	Tax @ 33%	Written down value c/f
1	400,000	100,000	33,000	300,000
2	300,000	75,000	24,750	225,000
3	225,000	56,250	18,563	168,750
4	168,750	42,188	13,922	126,562
5	126,562	—	—	—
Less:				
residual value	96,000			
	30,562 Balancing allowance		10,085	

Secondly we can then compute the present value of buying the asset.

Year	Cost	Tax relief	Net cash flow	Present value factor @ 8%	Present value
	£	£	£	£	£
0	(400,000)	—	(400,000)	—	(400,000)
1		—	—	0.92593	—
2		33,000	33,000	0.85734	28,292
3		24,750	24,750	0.79383	19,647
4		18,563	18,563	0.73503	13,644
5	96,000	13,922	109,922	0.68058	74,811
6		10,085	10,085	0.63017	6,355
					(£257,251)

Leasing

Year	Lease payment	Tax relief	Net cash flow	Present value factor @ 8%	Present value
	£	£	£	£	£
0	(100,000)	—	(100,000)	—	(100,000)
1	(100,000)	—	(100,000)	0.92593	(92,593)
2	(100,000)	33,000	(67,000)	0.85734	(57,442)
3	(100,000)	33,000	(67,000)	0.79383	(53,187)
4	(100,000)	33,000	(67,000)	0.73503	(49,247)
5	60,000 share of residual value	33,000	93,000	0.68058	63,294
6		33,000	13,200	0.63017	8,318
	Tax on residual value	(19,800)			(£280,857)

In this particular example, buying, taking into account 'the time value of money' would cost around £24,000 less than leasing the asset. However, it will not provide the 'hedge against obsolescence' which we looked at earlier in this chapter. The residual value of £96,000 is only an estimate, and could, because of advances in technology, be worth far less than that in 5 years' time.

Other factors worthy of note are that:

● The timing of the cash flows, i.e. when the money moves and/or the tax benefit is received (or the tax payment made), does affect the computations.
● There is usually a time lag, in practice, between claiming the benefits of taxation capital allowances and receiving the benefit. There is also a time lag between generating cash flows and paying tax on them.
● The system of capital allowances may change, e.g. to provide a higher rate of allowance for the year of purchase and then write off the remainder at 25 per cent reducing balance is just one of many possible alternative scenarios. In addition, the rates of tax could also change at some future date.

It cannot be said that purchasing outright is always cheaper than leasing and vice versa. It all depends upon the terms of the lease and the taxation effects applicable at the time.

SUMMARY

A lease takes place where one party, the lessor, hires out a specific asset such as a machine, equipment, property etc. to another party, the lessee who has the use of the asset for a specified period of time in exchange for rental payments as expressed in the terms of the lease.

A lease which transfers most of the risks and rewards of ownership to the lessee is called a '*finance lease*' or 'capital lease' or 'a full pay-out lease.' A lease in which the lessor retains most of the risks and rewards is called 'an operating lease' or 'a part-pay-out lease'.

The principle reasons why companies/organizations lease certain fixed assets are:

- it frees them from having to find a *'lump sum'*;
- the hope that the project will be 'self-financing', i.e. making lease payments out of the revenue generated;
- providing 'a hedge against obsolescence';
- once in force it cannot be withdrawn unless the terms are broken or by agreement of both parties;
- interest rates;
- taxation;
- an alternative to having to pledge assets as security or where loans are difficult/expensive because of the company's 'track record';
- the restrictive clauses may promote 'financial discipline';
- sale and leaseback to fund new projects.

For leases of land and buildings the lessee needs to look closely at the conditions of the lease such as:

- the term;
- the lump sum payable (if any);
- the amount of rent payable and the due dates;
- the frequency of rent reviews;
- details of any option to purchase;
- their responsibilities.

The lease versus buy decision can be computed via a number of methods/tabulations which use present value discount factors. Again, you should note that the information computed is just one part of the decision-making 'jigsaw'. You should also be aware that significant changes may take place in the tax capital allowances system, tax rates and that estimates of residual values of fixed assets in *n* years time may be way out!

Self-assessments

Now attempt these self-assessments to see how much of the chapter you have been able to digest. On completion compare your answers with the appropriate part of the chapter or for 10.5, with the answer which appears in Appendix 4 at the back of the book.

10.1   Quick short-answer questions

1   Explain the difference between a 'finance lease' and an 'operating lease'.
2   In connection with leasing, what is meant by 'providing a hedge against obsolescence'?

3 Provide an example of a 'restrictive clause' which could be found in certain leasing agreements.
4 How does 'sale and leaseback' work?
5 What is a long lease and what is a short lease in relation to land and buildings?

10.2

What are the advantages of leasing fixed assets other than land and buildings, and what are the drawbacks?

10.3

In the case of leasehold land and buildings what should a prospective lessee look out for in the proposed leasing agreement?

10.4

Describe, in your own words, the way in which the lease versus buy decision calculations were performed in this chapter.

10.5

You are provided with the following data relating to the purchase or lease of a new machine.

	Buying	Leasing
Cost	£320,000	£84,000 per year for 4 years
Residual value in 4 years' time	£160,000	£128,000 (for the lessee)

The after tax cost of borrowing is 10 per cent.

Taxation assumptions

● capital allowances at 25 per cent reducing balance;
● the rate of tax is 30 per cent;
● tax benefits will be received from year 2 onwards and can be fully utilized by the company.

Section IV

Evaluating performance

Chapter 11

Management and control of working capital

Objectives

When you have completed your review of this chapter you should then be in a position to:

- understand the criteria which have to be considered when deciding upon how much working capital a company should have;
- appreciate the need to control inventory, and
- describe the various items which comprise the costs of holding stocks and what management can do to reduce them;
- indicate how the amount of capital tied up in inventory may be reduced;
- explain briefly the costs involved in selling products (and services), on credit;
- discuss what credit control involves and how it can become more effective;
- appreciate the importance of finance from creditors;
- know why cash budgets are such an important part of working capital management;
- illustrate how to use appropriate ratios to analyse and review the working capital;
- describe the role of the auditor in the control of working capital.

WHAT IS WORKING CAPITAL?

Working capital, represents the difference between *current assets* and *current liabilities*. It provides an indication of the extent to which a business is able to meet its current obligations out of the assets which are held for conversion into cash.

Working capital = current assets − current liabilities

HOW MUCH WORKING CAPITAL SHOULD A COMPANY HAVE?

It is very difficult to lay down any hard and fast rules upon the amount of working capital needed (see Figure 11.1). The working capital requirements will

```
┌─────────────────────────────────────────────┐
│                                             │
│              The balance sheet               │
│                                             │
│              Capital employed:               │
│     Share capital + reserves + long-term debt│
│                                             │
└─────────────────────────────────────────────┘
                      ↕
┌─────────────────────────────────────────────┐
│                                             │
│               Represented by:                │
│          Fixed assets + investments          │
│             + working capital                │
│                                             │
└─────────────────────────────────────────────┘
```

Figure 11.1 Balance sheet relationships

vary from industry to industry, sector to sector and company to company. However, some of the following points must be borne in mind:

1   A certain percentage of the working capital is really a *fixed investment* and ought to be funded from long-term sources. A company will always tend to carry a certain volume of stocks and debtors.
2   Should the *bank overdraft* be treated as part of the working capital and included in the current liabilities? The fact that a bank overdraft may be called in at any time favours inclusion. If a company uses its bank overdraft as a long-term source of financing (and many companies do) it may be better to exclude the overdraft from the computation of working capital. This aspect is important, as it does affect the calculation of the liquidity ratios.
3   *Industry figures* will provide a yardstick with which a company can compare its own figures.
4   *Working capital budgeting.* This will take into account factors such as:
    (a)   the budgeted level of activity in terms of sales and production;
    (b)   the length of time that stocks are held as raw materials, work-in-progress and finished goods;
    (c)   the periods of credit received from suppliers and allowed to customers;
    (d)   the minimum acceptable cash and bank balances.
5   *The relationship between growth and working capital requirements.* Usually, if credit sales are increasing, this will dictate that working capital must also be increased. Supporting a higher volume of sales tends to call for an increase in working capital to provide for increased stocks and debtors.

INVENTORY

The costs of holding stocks

When asked the question 'How do people set a value on the cost of holding stocks?' one eminent purchasing executive replied, 'This is a question to which

I have never really found a satisfactory answer. I have posed the question to numerous accountants and the net result was one that could only be described as useless from the point of view of practical application.' It is rather surprising that many accountants are not particularly interested in this very important area especially when a substantial amount of working capital is tied up in stocks of materials and fuel, work-in-progress and finished goods.

In most industries the cost of material forms a significant part of the final selling price of the product. Management must not only strive to increase the productivity of labour but must also endeavour to increase the efficiency of material requirements planning (MRP) and thereby improve the productivity of capital. ROI (return on investment) is the real name of the business game. Other than increasing the selling price which may be sensitive to competition and external factors, materials management may, by direct inventory reduction and increased efficiency, play a part in increasing the productivity of the capital employed.

The principal aim of materials management is to keep stocks at an acceptably low level consistent with the risks involved. However, stockouts can cost the firm dearly in terms of lost production, idle time and lost orders. The setting of stock levels and levels of service must therefore involve a trade-off, hence the need for up-to-date information, continuous monitoring and frequent reviews.

Holding costs

What is the cost of holding stocks in your company and/or industry? A rule of thumb puts the cost of holding stock for one year in the region of 25p for every £1 of stock held. It must be remembered that there will most certainly be quite wide variations between the holding costs of companies and industries.

Which figures need to be included in the calculations of holding costs? It can be observed that holding costs include the costs of acquisition, storage, controlling, handling and rehandling, administration and others such as insurance and financial charges, and all these are in addition to the cost of the stocks held (see Figure 11.2).

Acquisition costs

One of the principal costs in the procurement of bought-out stock items is the cost of the purchasing function which is made up of staff wages and salaries,

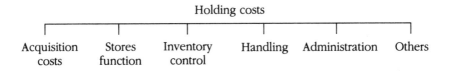

Figure 11.2 The costs involved in holding stocks

office accommodation, equipment and overheads, e.g. light and heat, fax and telephone, stationery. All the costs of ordering, finding suitable suppliers and negotiating terms should be included. Departmental costs of personnel and resources used for receiving and the inspection of goods inwards may also be classed as part of the acquisition costs.

The stores-warehouse function

The stocks of raw materials, work-in-progress and finished goods all take up valuable factory space in terms of expense and scarcity. Factory and office space is an extremely expensive commodity and must be utilized efficiently. The overheads associated with the space used for storage are many and include: rent and rates, insurance of buildings and equipment, light and heat, fire prevention, cleaning and maintenance. To this must be added the wages and salaries of stores and warehouse personnel. There is also a substantial investment in warehouse equipment such as bins and racks. In addition there are also losses attributable to shrinkage, deterioration, obsolescence and pilferage.

Inventory control

Considerable time and effort should be devoted to this area in order to keep stock levels to an acceptable minimum and thus bring about savings in holding costs. The costs applicable to this area involve material requirements planning, monitoring and review, the chief element being labour and computing costs. The expenditure upon internal audit related to stock control should also be included under this heading. The cost benefit of the system of inventory control should not be overlooked.

Handling

There could well be quite a hefty investment in handling equipment such as overhead cranes. In addition to the capital outlay for such equipment further expenditure has to be incurred to cover running costs, maintenance and servicing, e.g. drivers' wages, power, fuel and lubricants.

Administration

It may be more appropriate to include certain expenditure which could quite rightly appear under this heading, under some other heading, e.g. management of purchasing and material requirements planning. However, the costs of the financial and cost accounting recording systems for stocks acquired and/or issued and payments to suppliers must be accounted for.

Others

1 *Insurance.* Insurance premiums paid out to cover stock losses cannot be ignored. Insurance premiums are almost certain to rise when a firm increases the value of the stock it holds during the year. As pointed out earlier, insurance must also be taken to cover buildings and equipment, in addition to other risks, e.g. employer's liability and public liability.

2 *Set-up costs.* Where a company manufacturers some of its own components this involves a number of other costs in addition to the direct materials and labour, e.g. setting costs, machinery, patterns, and an appropriate share of overheads.

3 *Imported materials.* Various fees, duties, freight charges, and foreign exchange management costs relating to the importation of stock comprise yet another addition to the calculation of holding costs.

4 *The cost of capital.* Stock represents capital tied up in goods, and capital has to be paid for, with, e.g. interest charges and dividends. After all, it should be remembered that capital does have an opportunity cost.

5 *Stockout costs.* The cost of being out of stock can be very high in terms of lost production, sales, future orders and profit.

The calculation of a company's holding costs is not an impossibility. Holding costs can be identified and classified under a number of headings. Companies do keep an analysis of their payroll and materials used and should therefore be in a position to calculate with accuracy some of their holding costs. Overheads can be allocated and apportioned to departments or cost centres according to established cost accounting practice. It must be remembered that as stocks increase in volume, value and variety, the complexity of management planning and control also increases, and thus holding costs may escalate still further.

How can holding costs be reduced?

Inventory control and the reduction of holding costs

Stock represents 'capital tied up in goods': an old saying, but even more relevant in today's complex and diverse business environment. Thus, if stock holdings can be reduced, the amount of capital tied up can also be reduced. If the value and volume of stock held can be reduced, savings should be possible as follows:

1 *Interest charges.* Less capital tied up, less finance required for holding stocks.

2 *Storage space.* Less space required. Substantial savings in rent, rates, insurance, light, heat and personnel.

3 *Insurance.* Lower premiums to cover a lower value held in stock.

4 *Capital equipment requirements* and associated revenue expenditure reduced, e.g. running costs, interest charges.

5 *Handling.* Better utilization of capital equipment, e.g. more frequent deliveries. This area should be looked at very carefully, however, as handling charges in certain cases could increase.

How can the value and volume of stocks held be reduced?

There are several courses of action open to management. It is, however, appropriate at this point to stress the dangers of reducing stock levels. The first danger is that if this results in a 'stockout' the firm could be penalized for late delivery and lose future orders.

Secondly, the value of stocks held may appreciate in value in times of high inflation to such an extent that the stock appreciation exceeds the holding costs. Thirdly, if materials are ordered in smaller quantities and the frequency of delivery is increased, bulk discounts may be lost and certain handling charges increased. There is also cost benefit to consider. The cost of making savings in holding costs should not exceed those savings. Finally, remember that, there are no easy decisions in business, only trade-offs. What works for one firm may not work for another!

Reduction of material costs

To reduce the material costs, management may be able to:

1 *Obtain better discounts.* A small percentage increase in the discount could represent a vast sum of money.
2 *Improve production methods* to cut and/or eliminate waste; employees' suggestion schemes have been found to be very useful in this respect.
3 *Use less expensive materials* where this will not impair the function and/or required quality of the finished goods and services.
4 *Use standard components.* Variety is expensive and adds to the complexity of administration.
5 *New suppliers.* Search out new sources of supply via tenders, etc.
6 *Design.* Build in better utilization of materials at the design stage.

A reduction in inventory levels may be brought about by the following means:

Review of maximum, minimum and re-order levels

The stock levels referred to should be reviewed at frequent intervals in order to take account of seasonal fluctuations. In the real world the level of activity in the production departments will vary from week to week and/or from month to month. Therefore the stock levels should also vary, in an attempt to match materials requirements to production requirements. Some firms set maximum, minimum and re-order levels and then leave them in operation for periods in excess of one year!

The location of warehouses and stores

Where a company opts for a decentralized stores system it is quite probable that its inventory levels will be higher than they would be with a central stores system. The reason for this is simple. With a decentralized system the main stores and each sub-store will all have their own maximum, minimum and re-order levels. The decentralized systems also means increased complexity, e.g. increased paperwork and higher costs attributable to rehandling. The trade-off in this particular case is the time saved by having the stores in closer proximity to the production departments. However, the costs of having sub-stores in terms of space, equipment, personnel, and the capital tied up in stocks could far outweigh the benefits.

Pareto analysis

Twenty per cent of your stock could account for 80 per cent of the value.

Inventory management may find Pareto analysis a particularly valuable technique. If the 20 per cent mentioned above can be identified and subjected to extremely stringent control, management will, in fact, be controlling a very significant portion of its stock, that is, 80 per cent of the value of stock held. It may be possible to introduce a stock grading system which takes into account various factors such as value, importance to production, re-order period, and the level of service.

Regular deliveries and/or stock with short lead times

If stocks can be delivered on a regular basis, e.g. daily and/or weekly and go directly into the production process this reduces the raw material storage space required quite dramatically. This also applies to finished goods in cases where it is possible to dispatch daily and/or weekly to customers, for instance in the motor components industry. This type of system tends to come under the heading of JIT (just in time). In the case of stocks which can be obtained at relatively short notice, the risks of a stockout are not so serious. Why carry large stocks of materials which could be obtained at a moment's notice?

Sub-contractors and bought-out finished stock

The make or buy decision also has implications for holding costs. Rather than manufacture certain products or components it may be worthwhile using sub-contractors. The implications for the reduction of holding costs by employing the services of a sub-contractor are as follows:

- reduction of various items of stock needed to manufacture the product and/or component;
- less storage space needed;
- overheads are reduced, e.g. rent, lighting, administration;
- handling and re-handling is reduced;
- receiving department volume of work is cut;

- savings on equipment needed, e.g. handling and storage;
- purchasing effort simplified.

There are, however, additional savings to be gained because the production facilities are all provided by the sub-contractor. This means that the company concerned does not have to invest heavily in the machinery and factory capacity necessary to produce the product and/or component. The employment of sub-contractors can be described as 'a hedge against obsolescence'. The risk involved of machinery becoming obsolete or needing to be replaced rests firmly with the sub-contractor.

Design

More careful consideration at the design stage could improve materials utilization. Management must answer important questions relating to materials such as:

1 Which type of material should be used?
2 What else could be used in its place?
3 Should the operative working with the material be unskilled, semi-skilled or skilled?
4 Which of the plant and machinery is most suited to manufacturing the product?
5 Is it necessary to work to such very fine tolerances?

The type of material used certainly affects costs, but costs can also be affected by design weaknesses, the method of manufacture and the skills possessed by the operatives. Good design should ensure that the product can fulfil its function without using expensive materials unnecessarily and keep scrap and waste down to a minimum. Why use a bar made of brass when one made from cheap plastic would do exactly the same job without impairing the performance of the product?

Risk

The holding of stocks involves a certain degree of risk and high costs. The risks associated with stocks are that the product may not sell or fetch the anticipated price, stockouts, overstocking, pilferage, damage, waste and obsolescence, all of which may affect the firm's long-term stability. To reduce inventory levels frees capital for other purposes, reduces interest charges, and cuts the amount of expensive storage space required and the associated overheads.

Variety reduction and standardization

Variety of components stocked is expensive because it increases complexity, e.g. more administration. It is possible to achieve a variety of products using, where practicable, standard parts. The use of standard parts can effect a substantial reduction in the number of lines stocked and thus bring about a reduction in holding costs.

Example

A bus company had five different types of automatic doors. As a result it had to stock five different types of automatic door gears, each with its own maximum, minimum and re-order stock levels. The stock holding on this one item could have been reduced by a significant amount had the bus company decided to standardize the type of automatic door used on all of their buses. The use of standardized components, therefore, can bring about quite remarkable savings.

Coding and classification systems

Firms have been known to order stock from suppliers which they could have obtained from within their own stores. This situation highlights the fact that a firm really does need a satisfactory material classification system. Such a system should be capable of ascertaining whether particular items exist, and their location.

Surplus stocks

A strategy of surplus asset recognition and disposal (referred to in Chapter 4) also applies to inventory. Management must search out and identify obsolete and scrap items. This strategy will not only result in an inflow of cash to improve liquidity, but may also release valuable storage space, and contribute towards a significant reduction in overheads, e.g. insurance and other holding costs. The storage space vacated could be used to store materials for expanding product lines, or given over to production or may even be available for sale or sub-let. The same goes for capital equipment which is surplus to requirements. Why invest in assets which are seldom ever used and incur holding costs when the holding could be forever?

Operational research, statistical techniques and computers

If forecasting and control procedures are to be improved, management needs to become more familiar with operational research and statistical techniques such as simulation and modelling. Numerous computer packages are now available and management need to find out what such packages can do for them. This field alone provides great scope for improving materials management, e.g. matching stocks and production, and matching levels of service and the probability of a stockout.

Behavioural aspects

There is a tendency on the part of materials management to overstock, because running out of stock is considered by many to be a cardinal sin. This means that, in addition to carrying stocks which may not be required for some time, the firms concerned also have to cover certain holding costs unnecessarily. Stores kept on one side for a rainy day may, in fact, cost more in holding costs than their appreciation in value. Increased stock levels will, in addition to increasing holding costs, also increase risk. The attitude of 'thou shalt not run out of stock' needs changing to 'thou shalt ensure stocks are kept to an acceptable minimum'.

The role of audit

The internal and external auditors can help to detect and prevent errors and fraud and their contribution towards satisfactory control of materials should not be ignored. This important area will be dealt with in more depth later, on page 111.

Organization

In addition to investing in physical assets such as plant and machinery firms also need to invest in organization. Control systems, aided where necessary by computers, can help to reduce losses caused by inefficient uncoordinated systems, purchasing errors, deterioration, pilferage and obsolescence. If inventories are going to be managed efficiently and holding costs reduced it is imperative that all business functions co-operate, co-ordinate and communicate effectively.

Monitoring the environment

In today's complex and diverse business world it is essential to monitor the internal and external environment in which the firm operates. Monitoring the external environment, e.g. social, political, economic, technological, factor markets and product markets can assist the firm to identify threats and opportunities and enable it to respond to change more quickly.

Although management cannot and should not neglect efforts to improve the efficiency of plant and labour utilization, it must also ensure that the management of materials receives considerable attention. A total coherent approach is needed, for all business functions must work together to reduce the value of materials used and the associated holding costs.

The effect of inflation on stocks and the risk of a stockout should not be ignored. Decision-making in the real and imperfect world requires management that can see both sides of the argument and base decisions on the relevant facts, appreciating that trade-offs are inevitable.

Self-assessments 11.1

Attempt these self-assessments and then see how you compare with the appropriate sections of this chapter to date.

Explain in your own words, the answer to the question

1 How much working capital should a firm have?
2 Why is it that inventory can be described as 'capital tied up', and why is it so important to control it effectively?
3 What are 'inventory holding costs'?
4 How can management reduce their 'inventory holding costs'?

Short quick questions

1 Explain briefly the relationship between sales growth and working capital.
2 How can effective inventory control create more space?
3 What are the advantages of employing sub-contractors from the inventory control viewpoint?
4 Why can design improve material utilization?
5 How can monitoring the environment be an aid to effective inventory control?

The control of debtors (accounts receivable)

Often the quickest and best source of cash.

When a business sells goods, it may either demand immediate payment, i.e. cash sales, or it may permit payment to be made at a future date, i.e. credit sales. From the supplier's point of view, the benefits derived are the generation of sales or additional sales.

The cost of debtors

Question: Is it possible to determine the costs involved of selling on credit, i.e. the cost of the credit policy?
Answer: Yes. The costs concerned may be classified under the following three headings.

The cost of the capital used

Quite a number of questions need to be answered in this area, such as:

● What is the cost of capital that is tied up in debtors?
● What is the 'opportunity cost' of investing funds in debtors, e.g. interest lost?
● Has the firm sufficient funds to finance an increase in debtors, or must it seek funds from external sources?

- How long will the debts remain outstanding? (This will be made up of a combination of industry factors and customer variables.)
- Can the period of credit be reduced in any way, e.g. discounts or factoring?

The administration costs

- vetting applicants for credit sales;
- recording credit sales;
- credit control checks on customers at point of sale;
- processing credit sales for individual customer records;
- sending invoices to customers;
- sending statements to customers;
- chasing up slow paying customers;
- dealing with queries;
- recording receipt of cash and processing on individual customer records;
- use of office space, equipment and employees for the above tasks; note that the worse the customer, the more expensive the administration of their account.

The probability of non-payment

From the vetting procedure an estimate may be made of the likelihood of the customer eventually paying the debt. If a sufficiently large portfolio of customers exists, this can prove an accurate forecast of losses likely to arise from bad debts.

CREDIT CONTROL

The principal aim of effective credit control is to improve cash flow by reducing the average collection period and to keep bad debts to an acceptable level. It involves the following.

Credit screening

This involves determining the credit limits for each customer. Where can we find out about an applicant for trade credit?

- *Credit ratings and reports* by firms such as Dun and Bradstreet, etc. These are expensive.
- Company history. (For example, inspection of our own sales ledger.)
- Trade references. (However, these could be open to abuse.)
- Bank references. (Bankers may be unwilling to condemn their customer.)
- Financial statement analysis. (This could be out of date by the time it is available.)
- Salesperson's reports. (Remember that salespersons are not financial analysts.)

- *Involving salespersonnel* in the credit control process. (Remember that salespersons actually talk to customers at frequent intervals and may be able to provide valuable information.)

Aged analysis of debtors

This is usually a good starting point.

Prompt despatch of invoices and statements

This will reduce the time lag between delivery of the goods and payment. Many firms will not pay until they receive a statement. The frequency with which statements are sent out could be increased. Knowledge of your customers' payment systems could enable you to present invoices and/or statements in time for their next pay-out! The payment terms should be well publicised.

Chasing slow payers

A system of chasing slow payers could be via:

- Reminder letters.
- Phone calls and personal visits. (A single telephone call may quickly establish the reason why a particular debtor has not paid. The reason for non-payment could well be the supplier's own fault, e.g. relevant supplier's staff were not informed that the wrong quality was delivered to a customer because of a poor communication system.)
- Legal proceedings.
- Debt collection agencies.
- *Suspension of deliveries.* (This can damage goodwill.)
- *Discount for prompt payment.* (Some sectors of the economy have tried a late payment surcharge on delinquent accounts, but this could be unpopular and not highly successful.)

Salespersons

Salespersons receive a commission on sales and could on a number of occasions be guilty of selling to customers who are high credit risks. A salesperson is certainly not a financial analyst. However, some form of penalty, for example, a deduction from bonus earnings, related to the bad debts introduced by the salesperson merits attention.

Contra

It may be possible to buy something on credit from your debtor and simply offset the debt.

What else can be done?

- *Insure against bad debts.* Make someone else carry the risk, particularly if the extremes of probability would wipe the firm out. (This can be expensive.)
- *Factoring (with or without recourse).* Firms can get someone else to collect the debt for them, finance the waiting period, and sometimes also carry the risk of default. (This is also expensive, but sometimes necessary.)

Improving credit control

Improved credit control cannot only increase the cash flowing into the business but also reduce the amount of bad debts. What good is it if you make a sale but fail to ascertain the creditworthiness of your customer and don't get paid? How many credit controllers try to ascertain why a debtor has not paid? Frequently the reason for non-payment can be attributed to mistakes by the supplier, requiring some form of corrective action, e.g. sending a credit note to the customer concerned.

Self-assessments 11.2

Now make an attempt at each of these self-assessments and then see how your answer to each compares with the relevant material presented in this chapter.

1 What costs are associated with selling goods or services on credit?
2 Explain briefly what is meant by 'credit screening' and give examples of how we can find out more information about a prospective credit customer.
3 Describe briefly, four methods for chasing 'slow payers'.

Short quick questions

1 Under which three headings did we list the costs of selling on credit?
2 Why can it be useful to involve sales personnel in credit control?
3 How can the invoicing and sending out of statements system be improved so as to improve credit control?
4 In relation to credit control, how can a contra be used?

Finance from creditors

The time lag between the delivery of goods and the payment of suppliers may provide short-term finance. However, if discounts are offered in return for prompt payment, it could certainly be to a firm's advantage to pay promptly. The discount rate offered, although small, could, in fact, have a substantial effective annual rate of interest in excess of 20 per cent. It must be remembered that if firms place too much reliance upon finance from creditors this could cause their liquidity position to deteriorate.

Cash and bank balances

In addition to the usual everyday 'run of the mill', operating expenses and receipts, cash and bank balances may be affected quite considerably by a variety of factors, such as:

1   inventory holdings;
2   credit policy, e.g. terms available to customers;
3   the cash discounts and periods of credit granted by suppliers;
4   inflows of new capital;
5   capital expenditure;
6   dividend policy;
7   methods of distribution;
8   extraordinary items, e.g. losses on the conversion of foreign currency.

Internal control

To avoid losses arising from errors and fraud, particular attention will have to be paid to:

1   the whole system of cash recording; and
2   the physical handling of cash.

In both those areas, 'authority' is a key factor, such as the authority to write up the cash book via handwritten or computerized methods, and the authority to pay an invoice. (See also the role of audit in the control of working captial on page 111). For those who would like to find out more about this important area, reference can be made to auditing text books.

CASH BUDGETS

The pre-determination of cash balances fulfils a number of objectives, namely:

1   that cash is available in the appropriate amounts when required;
2   that cash shortages are highlighted well in advance, so that corrective action may be taken (see area X in Figure 11.3);
3   that cash surpluses are also highlighted and the possibility of investing them considered (see area Y in Figure 11.3).

The preparation of the cash budget (also called the cash flow forecast) involves:

1   taking into account the periods of credit allowed to debtors and granted by creditors for goods and services;
2   including the payments of dividends, taxation, capital expenditure, etc. in the month when the cash payment is expected to be made;
3   ignoring non-cash items such as depreciation.

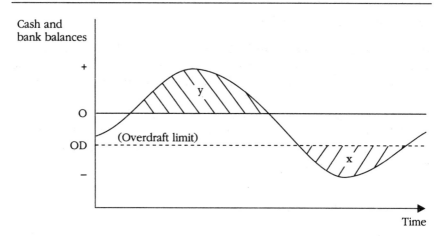

Figure 11.3 Cash graph

The key factor is the month in which the cash is expected to flow in or out, and not the period to which the receipt or payment relates.

The petty cash imprest system

The amount of the petty cash float is pre-determined, taking into account past experience and future developments. At the end of the period, whatever has been expended out of the petty cash will be reimbursed into petty cash. Thus, the new period will commence with the pre-determined balance. This is known as the 'imprest' system. It is an attempt to ensure that petty cash losses are limited.

Cash management: money market banking

One of the tasks of the 'treasury function' of larger companies is the investment of surplus funds on the money market. The chief characteristic of money market banking is one of size, a fact emphasized by the alternative description, 'wholesale' banking. Money market banks obtain funds by competing in the money market for the deposits of corporate customers, public authorities, wealthy individuals, and other banks. Deposits are made for specific periods ranging from overnight to one year, at highly competitive rates which reflect supply and demand on a daily, even hourly, basis. Consequently, the rates can fluctuate quite dramatically, especially for the shorter-term deposits. Even the most significant rate, the 3-month interbank rate, has fluctuated greatly over the years. Each day the previous day's rates are reported in the *Financial Times*, but bid deposit rates for substantial sums will be quoted by any bank upon request. The money market consists of accepting houses, British and foreign banks, and consortium banks.

Cash management: financial futures

The London International Financial Futures Exchange (LIFFE) enables companies to fix prices now for currency or a fixed interest commitment where the actual transaction will occur at some future date. (More information about this market may be obtained from LIFFE Ltd, Royal Exchange, London, EC3V 3PJ.) The exchange deals in currencies, 3-month Eurodollars, 3-month sterling and 20-year gilts etc. Companies may use the services provided by the exchange for hedging purposes, e.g. to reduce risk where they are vulnerable to changes in interest rates and exchange rates.

Cash management: foreign exchange management

Hedging against losses arising from currency fluctuations is an option which must be carefully considered by management. It is possible to buy and sell forward and in certain circumstances arrange currency swops.

THE ANALYSIS OF WORKING CAPITAL (RATIO ANALYSIS)

Ratio analysis enables comparisons to be made from year to year and with industry figures. This should help to identify areas of strength and pinpoint areas of weakness.

Tests of liquidity

Ratio of current assets or current liabilities (or current ratio)

This is used by the short-term lender to measure the company's ability to pay its obligations, and shows the margin of safety to meet unevenness in the flow of funds. For example:

$$\frac{\text{Current assets}}{\text{Current liabilities}} \quad \frac{£96,000}{£32,000} = 3:1$$

Liquid assets to current liabilities (quick ratio: liquid ratio or acid test ratio)

This measures the extent to which liquid resources are available to meet current demands. It shows also funds available for investment.

Liquid assets

This refers to cash; bank; debtors (see also Chapter 2).

Working capital ratio

$$\frac{\text{Working capital}}{\text{Net sales}} \quad \frac{64,000 \times 100}{200,000} = 32\%$$

This indicates how much additional working capital will be required to support an increase in selling capacity, e.g. £32 for every £100 sales.

Credit control

(a) Debtors average collection period (days): $\dfrac{\text{Average debtors} \times 365}{\text{Sales}}$

The *average* number of days taken by a debtor prior to settling the account.

(b) Debtors as % of sales: $\dfrac{\text{Average debtors} \times 100}{\text{Sales}}$

(c) Debtors turnover ratio: $\dfrac{\text{Sales}}{\text{Average debtors}}$

These three ratios all deal with the same relationship, but express the answer in different ways. (a) is the most common, and the most easily understood. (Note that when sales are a mixture of cash and credit, only the credit sales should be included in the above calculations.)

(d) Creditors, average payment period: $\dfrac{\text{Average creditors} \times 365}{\text{Cost of sales}}$

(e) The rate of stock turnover (or stock turn): $\dfrac{\text{Sales (or cost of sales)}}{\text{Average stock}}$

It shows the number of times the average stock held is sold in a given period.

Other aids

In addition to the techniques already mentioned in this chapter, there are a number of useful aids to the control and management of working capital. These are as follows:

- *Variance analysis*, via budgetary control or standard costing. Action taken on the basis of the information provided and can most certainly lead to improvements in cash flow and inventory management.
- *Control accounts* provide an arithmetic proof of the stock and the debtor balances.
- *Funds flow statements* drawn up to explain what has happened to working capital. These are not to be confused with cash flow statements prepared for financial accounting purposes.

The profit and loss account and balance sheet of a company show the amount of profit (or loss) made during the year and the disposition of the company's resources at the beginning and at the end of the year. However, for a fuller understanding of a company's affairs it is necessary also to identify movements in assets, liabilities and capital which have taken place during the year and the resultant effect upon working capital.

THE ROLE OF AUDIT IN THE CONTROL OF WORKING CAPITAL

The objects of an audit

An Auditor is a Watchdog not a Bloodhound (Kingston Cotton Mills Case, 1896)!

The aim of an audit is to verify and report upon the financial state of an organization, (providing a true and fair view), and to detect and prevent errors and fraud.

Various classes of audit

1   statutory, e.g. companies; building societies;
2   private firms (by letters of appointment);
3   trust accounts;
4   partnerships (partnership agreement);
5   internal audit (employees of the company or firm).

An outline of the work of an auditor (VEREC or verec)

- *Verify the existence, ownership* and *basis of valuation* of the assets, and ensure that the liabilities are fully and accurately disclosed.
- *Examine* vouchers and any other evidence (e.g. collateral evidence), that may be required to prove that the entries in the books of account are complete and authentic.
- *Report* to the proprietors whether the balance sheet shows a true and fair view of the affairs, and the profit and loss account a true and fair view of the profit or loss for the financial period under review.
- *Enquire as to the authority* for transactions (e.g. ordering of goods, purchase of fixed assets, petty cash payments, signing of cheques and contracts, and see that all benefits which should have been accounted for have, in fact, been received. Obtain satisfactory explanations to enquiries.
- *Check* the arithmetical accuracy of the books of account and that the systems of internal control are working effectively.

Internal control

This covers not only the internal check and internal audit but the whole system of controls, financial or otherwise, established by the management in order to carry on the business of the enterprise in an orderly and efficient manner, safeguard the assets and secure, as far as possible, the accuracy and reliability of its records.

Internal check

This involves the checks on day-to-day transactions which operate continuously as part of the routine system whereby the work of one person is proved independently, or is complementary to the work of another (i.e. the 'who done it!'). The object is the prevention or early detection of errors or fraud.

Internal audit

This means a review of operations and records, sometimes continuous, undertaken within a business by specially assigned staff.

Auditing in depth

This is the procedure by which the auditor assesses the efficiency of the system of internal control. It involves tracing a transaction through various stages from its *origin to conclusion*, and examining at each stage to an appropriate extent the vouchers, records and authorities relating to that particular stage and observing the incidence of internal check and delegated authority.

The role of internal and external audit in the control and management of fixed assets and working capital should not be under-estimated. It is the responsibility of management to ensure that adequate systems of internal control are in operation. It is the task of the auditors to assess the efficiency of those systems and to inform management of any possible weaknesses. In this way losses due to errors and fraud should be minimized.

SUMMARY

The inventory and debtors figures which appear in a firm's balance sheet could well include 'hidden capital'. Unfortunately, this can be a direct consequence of inefficiency, and management may be reluctant to put right a situation for which they are responsible. Management must strive to reduce stock holdings (without endangering the flow of production) as this will reduce the capital invested in stocks, release valuable factory space and possibly reduce overheads.

Improvements in credit control vetting and collecting procedures is considered to be one of the quickest ways of generating cash. The costs of improving inventory control and credit control must not exceed the benefits to be derived from instituting those improvements. It is a most unsatisfactory state of affairs which permits debtors to avoid payment simply because the cost of collection exceeds the amount outstanding.

The constantly changing environment in which the firm operates dictates that management must always keep a watchful eye on whether or not it is worthwhile to insure against bad debts, make use of debt factoring, or using book debts as security for a loan.

The role of internal audit (and indeed external audit) should not be under-estimated in the control of working capital and the generation of internal finance. By ensuring that adequate systems of internal control are instituted and operating correctly, losses due to errors and fraud can be minimized. The prevention and detection of error and fraud is particularly important in the areas of inventory and debtors. Random stock checks and vetting of authorization procedures certainly have a moral effect upon employees. Internal control is a management responsibility.

Efficient control of working capital = Improved productivity of capital

Self-assessments 11.3

Attempt the following self-assessments and then compare your attempt with the information provided in this chapter.

1 'Verec' is a mnemonic which describes the role of an auditor. Explain what it means.
2 In relation to auditing, what is meant by:
    (a) 'internal control'; and
    (b) 'auditing in depth'?

Short quick questions

1 Why is it usually wise to take advantage of a discount offered by suppliers for prompt payment of 'an invoice'?
2 What is the purpose of a cash budget?
3 Define in your own words, what a 'petty cash imprest' is?
4 Explain briefly the role of the 'treasury function' re money market banking.

Further reading

Chadwick, L. (1980) Should we be more inward looking – for that extra finance, *Management Accounting*, February.
Houlihan, J.B.S. (1978) Proceedings of the 13th BPICS European Technical Conference. *Management Accounting: Official Terminology* (1982) London: CIMA.
Muhlemann, A., Oakland, J. and Lockyer, K. (1992) *Production and Operations Management*, London: Pitman.

Ray, D.L. (1980) 'Inventory management performance must improve', *Purchasing and Supply Management*, April.

Weston, J.F. and Brigham, E.F. (1988) *Managerial Finance* (British edition) London: Cassell.

Woodward, H.N. (1976) 'Management strategies for small companies', *Harvard Business Review*, January/February. (Also published in *Certified Accountant*, August 1976).

Chapter 12

Dividend policy

Objectives

When you have read this chapter you should be able to:

- recognize the importance of a declared dividend policy;
- calculate pay-out ratios;
- understand some of the legal constraints associated with dividends;
- identify inter-relationships with the financing and investment decisions considered so far.

INTRODUCTION

Dividends paid represent a cash outflow on the cash flow statement. The payment of dividends depletes the cash resources, but the payment of a scrip dividend (or bonus issue) avoids the use of cash. Dividend policy is complementary to retention policy. Retentions are used to finance capital projects and redeem shares and debentures. Actually, it is the assets underpinning these reserves that are used. It should also be remembered that retentions are part of equity and therefore enter into the cost of capital calculation. Dividends may have an effect on the value of the company's shares, which in turn could affect the cost of capital when the model $\frac{d}{p} + g$ is used.

There is also the problem of whether to pay an interim dividend in addition to the final dividend and if the rate of dividend is increased, whether it can be maintained in the future. Thus dividend policy impinges on a number of different aspects of financial management.

LEGAL AND OTHER CONSIDERATIONS

There are several legal considerations affecting the distribution of dividends, which include the following:

1 Dividends can only be paid out of profits. Under no circumstances can shareholders' capital be returned to them disguised as dividends.

2   Preference shareholders usually have a prior right to dividend.
3   Shareholders have no entitlement to dividend until it is declared and approved at the Annual General Meeting.
4   Capital profits may only be used for dividend where the Articles permit and there is a bona fide revaluation of all the assets of the company. The profit has to be converted into cash, i.e. realized.
5   If the company fails to pay a dividend it may lose its status as a trustee investment under the Trustee Investment Act 1961.

Additional factors

Other additional factors need to be considered. These are as follows.

Taxation

Dividends received by the shareholder are paid net of tax, with the shareholder receiving a tax credit. The company has to pay advanced corporation tax, which may be offset against its corporation tax liability, but the date of payment is brought forward to 3 months after the date of payment of the dividend. This has an effect on the cash flow and may cause liquidity problems.

Government controls

Any dividend controls under a wages and incomes policy, restricting the level of dividends, must be adhered to.

Shareholders' needs and preferences

Certain shareholders, e.g. senior citizens, are dependent upon dividends as a major source of income. An alteration in dividend policy may adversely affect them. In addition, the institutional investors usually require dividends in order to meet their commitments.

Pay-out ratios

The stability of dividends is most important, whereby the level of dividend is only increased when the company is reasonably certain that the level of profits underpinning the dividend can be maintained. This means that there is a time lag between the earning of profits and the payment of dividends.

Companies usually set a target pay-out ratio, expressed as follows:

$$\frac{\text{Dividend per share}}{\text{Earnings per share}}$$

This ratio level then becomes the target and as profits increase the level of dividend increases accordingly. If the target ratio was 0.33 then the shareholder would receive one-third of the available profit, with two-thirds being retained for future growth, and presumably invested in worthwhile capital projects.

Accordingly, the level of the pay-out ratio is somewhat dependent upon the level of anticipated investment projects. Once the company knows its long-term investment requirements it can plan its long-term dividend pay-out ratio.

Self-assessment 12.1

Calculate the dividend pay-out ratio from the following data:

Ordinary issued share capital	
10,000 shares of 50p each, fully paid	£5,000
Undistributed profits	
Brought forward	9,000
After tax profit for current year	3,000

The directors are considering a dividend of £900.

OTHER FACTORS RELATING TO DIVIDEND POLICY

It is important that a company has a specific dividend policy and declares it. Shareholders who prefer that kind of policy will be attracted. This is known as the 'clientele effect'. The company should then continue with that policy into the future, otherwise the shareholders will become aggrieved. It is also important to know who its shareholders are and determine their needs and preferences. Having set the policy, additional dividends may be paid, over and above the normal, provided that they are stated as such.

Self-assessment 12.2

Discuss the factors which should be taken into account when formulating the dividend policy of a company.

Self-assessment 12.3

What would be the implications for a company which had a dividend pay-out ratio of 90 per cent?

SUMMARY

In this chapter you have been made aware of the implications attaching to the dividend decision. Payment of dividends involves an outflow of cash which might be better deployed in worthwhile capital projects, generating positive net present values. In this way the shareholders' wealth might be truly maximized. In addition, once the dividend policy has been established, it should be announced and adhered to. The stability of dividend is a most important consideration.

Further reading

Brealey, R. and Myers, S. (1991) *Principles of Corporate Finance*, London: McGraw Hill.
Weston, J.F. and Copeland, T.E. (1988) *Managerial Finance*, London: Cassell.

Chapter 13

Share valuation

Objectives

When you have read this chapter you should be able to:

- name three bases used to value ordinary shares;
- calculate share values using those bases;
- understand why a controlling interest is worth more than one without control;
- value preference shares.

INTRODUCTION

This topic interacts with the areas of dividend policy, capital budgeting, rates of return and the capital structure decision. Accounting traditionally uses the lower of cost or net realizable value for valuation purposes. This is inappropriate for purchase and sale decisions as it does not reflect the current value. A share is a part of the net assets of a business, i.e. an investment therein. The value of a share is a function of what the business/shares will be earning in the future, which can be described as the present value of the future income stream. Unfortunately the future is uncertain, therefore valuations will differ.

The price of a share is dependent upon the following:

1 supply and demand forces;
2 the state of the economy;
3 shareholder preferences and expectations.

Supply is controlled by the company in the first instance when it decides on the number of shares to be issued. Today there are many share dealings on the Stock Exchange in shares which were issued years ago. Demand for the shares is subject to the success of the company and how well it communicates that success to the stock market. Success is measured by earnings, dividends, growth, and rates of return.

METHODS OF SHARE VALUATION

Methods used in the valuation of shares are based upon net assets, earnings and dividends.

Net assets basis

This method uses the total assets (suitably re-valued) less the liabilities, i.e. the net assets. The net assets are the same as the equity of the company where there are no preference shares. Therefore we are effectively arriving at a value of the equity.

Self-assessment 13.1

Define equity.

Illustration

The following balance sheet refers to Elmtree Ltd. The asset values have been adjusted to take account of current circumstances.

Fixed assets	£150,000
Current assets	35,000
	185,000
Current liabilities	10,000
	175,000
50,000 ordinary shares	50,000
Reserves	125,000
	175,000

Determine the value per ordinary share.

Goodwill ought to be included in the value of total assets, but for now it is to be ignored. The net assets of £175,000 are divided by the number of ordinary shares of 50,000. The share value based on net assets is £3.50 per share.

Dividend yield basis

The yield, a rate of return using dividends, is calculated as follows:

$$\text{Dividend yield} = \frac{\text{Dividend per share}}{\text{Market price per share}} \times 100$$

Obviously we cannot determine both the market value and the yield where both are unknown. In this case an assumed yield is substituted based on similar businesses.

Illustration

Elmtree Ltd has paid a dividend of £12,500 on its ordinary shares. A dividend yield of 6 per cent is considered to be adequate. Calculate the share value.

Dividend per share: 12,500/50,000 = 25p

$$6\% = 25p/MPPS$$
$$MPPS = 0.25/0.06 \qquad = £4.16$$

It should be recognized that the dividend policy of a company is crucial to the valuation under this method. Government dividend controls would also affect the valuation. It is also true that past dividend levels will not necessarily be continued into the future. For all these reasons the use of this basis can be criticized.

Earnings yield basis

To overcome the problems associated with dividends, the yield based upon earnings can be used. It can also be used for unquoted shares and new issues. With this method the earnings per share (EPS) is multiplied by a relevant price earnings ratio (P/E).

Illustration

The earnings of Elmtree Ltd (i.e. profits available to the ordinary shareholders after tax) amounted to £30,000. A relevant P/E ratio, which takes account of expected dividends plus retentions, is 7, represented by the sector of industry in which Elmtree operates. Calculate the share value.

EPS: £30,000/50,000 = 60p per share
P/E × EPS = 60p × 7 = £4.20

Note the problem of obtaining the relevant P/E ratio, particularly for a company operating in two or three industrial sectors, e.g. Boots Plc.

Self-assessment 13.2

The following details have been extracted from the accounts of Townend Ltd.

Profit and loss account	
Sales	£2.4m
Less: Cost of sales	1.4
	1.0
Less: Selling, distribution and administration expenses	0.76
Net profit	0.24
Less: Dividend for the year	0.12
	0.12

Add: retained earnings brought forward		0.60
Retained earnings carried forward		0.72
Balance sheet		
Freehold premises at cost		0.20
Less: depreciation		0.02
		0.18
Motor vehicles	0.60	
Less: depreciation	0.40	0.20
Stock in trade		0.40
Debtors and prepayments		0.60
Cash at bank		0.02
		1.40
Ordinary shares of £1 each		0.20
Reserves		0.72
Creditors and accruals		0.48
		1.40

The freehold premises are to be valued at £0.76m.

Required

Calculate the value of the shares using net assets, dividends and earnings. Ignore goodwill. Companies operating in the same sector of industry as Townend Ltd have a P/E of 9 and a dividend yield of 7.5 per cent.

Controlling interests

A controlling interest exists where a shareholder holds more than 50 per cent of the ordinary share capital of a company. Such a shareholder has the power to run the company through voting control. That is to say, such a shareholder can influence decisions relating to such key areas as capital budgets, capital structure and dividends. Therefore this shareholding is valued higher than one without control.

Self-assessment 13.3

Brian Townend has a controlling interest in Towend Ltd. What value would you suggest for each share that he holds?

Preference shares

The valuation of preference shares depends on whether the preference shares are cumulative or participating. The valuation is based upon the fixed rate of dividend (called the coupon rate) and the expected yield.

Dividend per share = Coupon rate × Nominal value per share
Share value   = Dividend per share/expected yield

This is the same as the basis used for dividends above.

Self-assessment 13.4

You are required to calculate the valuation of a preference share in Laurel Ltd, given the following information.

200,000 6% preference shares of £1 each: £200,000

The expected yield from such securities is currently 8 per cent.

Conclusion

It can be seen that the value of the shares of Elmtree Ltd based upon assets, dividends and earnings leads to a range of values rather than one precise figure. This is not unusual. What we are able to ascertain is that the value falls between £3.50 and £4.20. A seller of shares would be hoping to obtain £4.20, but a buyer would be looking to pay £3.50. In the end, the value would be what the buyer was prepared to pay and the seller accept.

SUMMARY

This chapter has dealt with three bases for the valuation of shares, i.e. net assets, dividend yield and earnings yield. There are problems associated with each. These include the valuation of assets, including off the balance sheet assets such as goodwill, and the selection of an appropriate dividend yield and price earnings ratio. As a result the valuations are subjective.

Further reading

Samuels, J.M. and Wilkes, F.M. (1995) *Management of Company Finance*, Wokingham: Van Nostrand Reinhold.

Section V

Control

Chapter 14

Budgets and budgetary control

This chapter does not aim at being the type of chapter which you may or could encounter in a management accounting-type text. It is not a number crunching-type chapter; it is a chapter which is designed to provide you with a concise enunciation of the cardinal principles.

Objectives

When you have finished reading this chapter and completed all of the self-check assessments you should be able to:

1 Know what is involved in the budget preparation process, and in particular the importance of:
   - the co-ordinator;
   - the time table;
   - meetings;
   - participation;
   - inter-dependence;
   - the 'master budget';
   - the 'principal budget factor';
   - capital expenditure budgets;
   - cash budgets and the 'treasury function'.
2 Understand how control is achieved via:
   - control by responsibility;
   - continuous comparison;
   - 'management by exception';
   - flexible budgets, and
   - zero-based budgeting (ZBB);
   - taking behavioural factors into account, and
   - monitoring and revising budgets.

BUDGETING

CIMA (The Chartered Institute of Management Accountants) have defined a budget as:

> A plan expressed in money. It is prepared and approved prior to the budget period and may show income, expenditure, and the capital to be employed. May be drawn up showing incremental effects on former budgeted or actual figures, or be compiled using zero-based budgeting.

Budget preparation

The budget preparation process involves appointing someone to *co-ordinate* it, e.g. an accountant, and to draw up and circulate to appropriate personnel, a budget preparation *time table*.

The co-ordinator's role involves, linking up with the top management, communications, organizing and chairing various *meetings*, providing data to those charged with the task of preparing estimates and setting targets. It is an important principle worthy of note, that all those who should be involved, including junior managers, supervisors and 'shop floor' workers, *participate* in the budget preparation process. Some of their views and advice could save the company/organization thousands of pounds.

The time table would provide the dates of the various meetings and dates for the submission of estimates, tabulations, reports, feedback, etc. The *preparation in advance* means that assumptions about the future have to be made, e.g. the rate of inflation, trading conditions, legislation, foreign exchange etc. Information from the past, although not always a good guide to the future, can help, together with information about the future such as expected trends, reports, government statistics etc. in the pre-determination of the budgets. However, it should also be remembered that budgets are *targets* for *control* purposes, e.g. sales targets, spending targets, production targets etc. Thus, the budgets (*targets*) set should be *realistic and achievable*. Budgets will be prepared for both the short term and the long term for each *budget centre*. A budget centre being a section or department of an organization, e.g. a production department or group of similar machines, the security function and the stores function.

Inter-dependence

Individual budgets cannot be set without reference to other budgets. Budgets are *inter-related* and what happens in one budget may affect one or more of the other budgets. It is most important therefore, that if the budgeting system is going to be effective, there must be:

- clear *communications*;
- good *co-ordination*; and
- *meetings*.

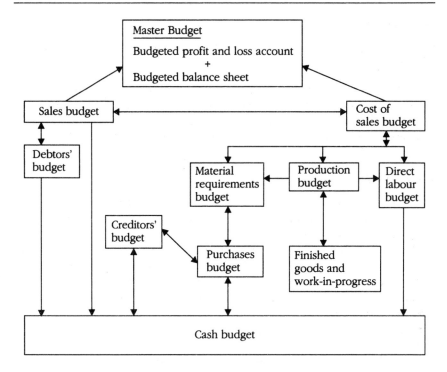

Figure 14.1   Budgetary inter-dependence and the cost of sales budget

The meetings should involve appropriate personnel from the various functions to discuss factors which affect their budget, targets, problems and matters of common interest. We will take the budgeted cost of sales, as illustrated in Figure 14.1 as an example of the inter-dependence between budgets. You should observe that there is a link between the sales budget and the cost of sales budget. The sales budget is usually the starting point of the budget preparation process, as it has a very strong influence in determining the '*level of activity*', i.e. the output, which is needed to match up with the sales targets.

The sales budget helps to set the production budget after taking account of budgeted opening and closing stocks of finished products and work-in-progress. The material requirements budget assists in the setting of the purchases budget after taking account of budgeted opening and closing stocks of raw materials. The direct labour budget is influenced by the production budget, and so on. Many of the budgets illustrated also affect the cash budget. The end product is the *master budget* which usually consists of a budgeted trading and profit and loss account (P&L account) and a budgeted balance sheet. Thus, the budget preparation process is rather like a large 'jigsaw' and a 'balancing act' because it does involve the sharing out and utilization of the company/organization's scarce resources. It is essential that all the pieces of this jigsaw fit together to form a coherent plan which is sensible and workable.

THE PRINCIPAL BUDGET FACTOR

You will recall, that the usual starting point for the budget preparation is the sales budget. However, this is only the case if there is no principal budget factor (also called limiting factor or key factor) which constrains what can or cannot be done. It is the factor which has to be taken into account first as it limits the company/organization's level of activity. For example, if production capacity is the principal budget factor, and only a certain number of products can be produced in a specified period, then taking into account budgeted opening and closing stocks, there is a limit to the number of products available for sale. You cannot sell more than you can produce!

Management can take action to reduce the effect of, or eliminate the principal budget factor. For example, production capacity problems can be overcome by:

- working longer hours, e.g. overtime, shift work;
- introducing an incentive scheme, to make more in the time available;
- acquire more machinery and production equipment;
- improve production planning to cut down on 'idle time' and avoid 'bottle necks';
- use sub-contractors to produce certain products;
- buy some of the components, which are made internally, from outside suppliers.

Other principal budget factors which management are likely to come across are sales demand, the supply of labour, availability of finance and governmental legislation.

Capital expenditure budgets

In addition to the functional budgets such as the sales budget, the production budget, and the research and development budget another very important budget is the capital expenditure budget. Budgets will have to be drawn up relating to capital expenditure for items such as:

- new fixed assets e.g. land, buildings, machinery, equipment and vehicles;
- permanent increases in working capital which have to be financed from long-term sources.
- the redemption of preference shares and debentures or the repayment of loans.

Assessing and sorting out the capital expenditure will no doubt involve: the evaluation of proposals, numerous meetings, screening, trade-offs and compromise, re-vamping proposals, re-assessments and authorization. In addition, a financing budget will also need to be drawn up to plan where all the money needed to fund the capital expenditure is coming from. Here also, the budgets are inter-related to various other budgets, e.g. the capital expenditure could include new machines so that the production budget can be achieved. The way in which it is funded will affect the finance budget and cash budget.

Cash budgets (cash flow forecast)

A cash budget is drafted to show when the cash actually moves, i.e. when it comes in and when it goes out. Its purpose is to see that cash is available when it is needed and to highlight surpluses and shortages. It is a very useful aid when it comes to the control and management of working capital, see Chapter 11. Of particular importance to financial management is the *treasury function*, which involves putting surplus cash balances to work for short periods which could be for overnight or two or three months. This increases the productivity of the capital employed, in that money is not just lying idle in a bank current account but earning some interest.

Self-assessments 14.1

When you have attempted each of the following self check assessments, compare your attempt with the appropriate part of this chapter.

1 What are the essential features of the budget preparation process?
2 Why is 'participation' such an important part of the budget preparation process?
3 Explain why budgets cannot be prepared in isolation of each other.
4 What is a 'principal budget factor' and how can management reduce its impact?
5 Explain briefly the possible problems which have to be faced when drawing up the capital expenditure budget.

Short, quick questions

(These can be answered in two or three lines)

1 What does the budget co-ordinator's job entail?
2 Why should targets be realistic and achievable?
3 What is a 'master budget'?
4 The sales budget is not always the starting point of the budget preparation process. Why?
5 How can the 'treasury function' improve the productivity of the capital employed?

BUDGETARY CONTROL

CIMA (the Chartered Institute of Management Accountants) define budgetary control in their official terminology as:

> The *establishment of budgets* relating the *responsibilities of executives* to the *requirements of a policy*, and the *continuous comparison* of actual with budget results, either to secure by individual *action* the *objectives* of that policy or to *provide a basis for its revision.*

This definition has stood the test of time and has changed very little over the years, as it does incorporate the essential components necessary to achieve effective control.

The establishment of budgets

This involves planning for the short term and the long term, and takes up a lot of time, thought, discussion, co-operation, communications and co-ordination, as indicated earlier in this chapter.

Control by responsibility

Control is exercised by making an individual, e.g. a director, manager or supervisor, responsible for a particular budget or sub-section of a budget. For example, a supervisor for a group of machines could be responsible for the production budget relating to those machines, whereas overall responsibility for the production budget could be in the hands of the production director. All these people, who are responsible for a budget or a sub-section of the budget, should be actively involved in the budget preparation process, including the setting of targets where appropriate. In addition, they may be called upon to explain why targets have not been achieved.

Policy requirements

The policy to be followed should be formulated and agreed upon by the top management, hopefully with inputs from all levels of management and worker representatives. It is designed with a view to making sure that the objectives set are achieved. There will be policies for all functions, e.g. a sales policy, a production policy, a personnel policy etc. This will impact upon the various budgets and control data, e.g. assessment as to whether or not the policy/policies is/are working.

Continuous comparison

For control purposes variances between the actual results and the budget should be reported at regular intervals. The statements should be designed to highlight significant adverse variances and also provide an explanation as to why the variance has happened. Armed with this information, management can devote their attention to those items highlighted and take appropriate *corrective action*. This system, designed to enable management to focus their time, energy, skills and talents on matters which really do need their consideration, is known as '*management by exception*' and '*exception reporting*'.

Flexible budgets

If control is to be effective, it is important that flexible budgets, i.e. those which change in line with the level of activity are used. A fair comparison can only be made if the actual level of activity is compared with a budget which has been computed for the same level of activity. We must compare like with like, otherwise the variances calculated will be meaningless. The alternative to a flexible budget is a fixed budget which is of no use for control purposes.

Zero-based budgeting (ZBB)

ZBB has been found useful in the services and support areas. Rather than using last year plus a percentage, i.e. incremental budgeting, all ZBB budgets start from a nil base. Managers who are involved in such a system have to *justify and rank* all of their proposals. It aims at bringing about a fairer allocation of scarce resources between competing factions/proposals.

Behavioural factors

Budgetary control is an attempt to ensure that the objectives of the company/organization are achieved. It is not supposed to be a 'whipping post', i.e. taking the blame for everything that goes wrong. It is not designed as a device by which those responsible for budgets/sub-sections of budgets are to be reprimanded. The perception of what the budget is, and is trying to do will vary with each individual involved in the system, unless they receive appropriate '*budget education*'.

However, individuals, being quite complex beings, do have perceptions and their own goals. These goals may conflict with their company's/organization's own objectives. Behavioural factors cannot, and should not be ignored. To ignore them, could cost the company/organization dearly.

Monitoring

The budgets set are *only estimates* based upon the best available information at the time of their conception. The assumptions on which the budgets were based must be monitored. If the assumptions are affected by significant changes, then those budgets which are affected will need to be *revised*.

Self-assessments 14.2

When you have had a go at answering these self checks, see how your attempt compares with the information provided in this chapter.

1 Explain what is meant by 'control by responsibility' in relation to budgetary control.
2 How should the statements which report the variances between budget and actual figures be designed so as to enable management to focus their time and energy on matters which are not going according to plan?

Short quick questions

(Answers should only take up two or three lines.)

1 Provide an example of 'control by responsibility'.
2 Why is it important to use flexible budgets?
3 ZBB, is considered to be a fairer way of allocating resources, particularly in the services and support area. Why?
4 How can a budget education programme help to reduce behavioural problems associated with budgeting and budgetary control?

SUMMARY

The budget preparation process should be carefully and effectively co-ordinated and involve keeping to the preparation time table. It should also include a number of meetings which involve all the personnel, both junior and senior, who should be consulted and involved. Participation, is an essential ingredient if the budgeting system is to be a success. Budgets cannot be constructed independently of each other as they are inter-related. What happens in one area will tend to affect the budgets of one or more other areas, see Figure 14.1.

The usual starting point in the budget preparation process is the sales budget. This, however, is not the case if there is a 'principal budget factor', other than sales, which limits what can or cannot be done, for example if materials are limited in supply for a specified period. You will recall, that the principal budget factor's effect can be reduced or eliminated via management taking appropriate corrective action. Control by responsibility means that an individual will be in charge of a budget or a sub-section of a budget. For example a sales area manager would be responsible for the sales target for their area and for explaining variances between the budgeted and actual performance.

Comparison of budget/actual figures should be carried out at frequent intervals. This provides management with an *early warning* and *early detection* system of matters that are not going according to plan. The reports will be hopefully designed to highlight significant adverse variances together with details of why they have happened. ZBB (zero-based budgeting) has been found to be useful in the services and support areas of business. The behavioural aspects of budgeting can never be ignored, e.g. if the targets set are too high or too low, employees' reactions may prove to be very costly to the organization concerned. Finally, budgets are only estimates, if the assumptions on which they were based change significantly, then the budgets must be revised accordingly.

Suggested projects

1   Draft a budget preparation time table for a manufacturing company.
2   Prepare a job specification for a 'budget co-ordinator'.
3   Seek out and describe examples of 'good participation' and 'bad participation' in the budgeting preparation process.
4   Explain the link between the capital expenditure budget and capital budgeting, a name used to describe capital investment appraisal.
5   What kind of budgeting problems would you expect to encounter in a large organization such as the BBC (British Broadcasting Corporation)?
6   What action can management take where their 'principal budget factor' is the availability of finance?

Further reading

Chadwick L. (1993) *Management Accounting* (Elements of Business series) London and New York: Routledge.

Chapter 15

Strategic management

Objectives

This chapter is designed to give you a foundation level appreciation of the subject area. When you have digested its contents you should be able to:

- list some of the principal activities with which strategic management is concerned;
- understand how the corporate planning process may take place;
- explain about the areas to which the monitoring activities should be extended, in both the internal and external environment in which the company/organization operates;
- discuss briefly how behavioural factors, such as, 'gate-keeping' and 'political access' can affect decision-making within the corporate structure.

WHAT IS STRATEGIC MANAGEMENT?

> Strategy is when you are out of ammunition, but keep on firing so that the enemy will not know! (Ansoff)

> The overall problem of business is to configure and direct the resource-conversion process in such a way as to optimise the attainment of objectives. (Cyert and March)

Strategic management, it has been said, is concerned with the effect of current decisions upon the long-term performance of an undertaking. It is however, much more than this. Strategic management is concerned with the following:

- the setting of corporate objectives, and
- the formulation of the policy to be followed in order to achieve those objectives;
- the provision and allocation of resources, e.g. budgetary control. The budget system, by being recognized as the articulation in financial terms of the plans of an organization, is a most effective method for implementing strategy;
- ensuring long-term progress and survival;

- the search for and selection of alternative courses of action and weighing up items such as trade-offs and cost benefit;
- communicating objectives, policies and plans effectively in order to promote teamwork, responsibility and appropriate action. This demands an efficient information system which not only communicates throughout the organization, but also provides for feedback on a continuing basis;
- managing risk and uncertainty. Plans must also take into account, what happens if things go wrong? Plans must be reviewed at regular intervals.
- analysis of performance, e.g. the provision of yardsticks;
- monitoring the environment in which the organization operates;
- setting up the organizational structure necessary for the speedy implementation of managerial decisions;
- making sure that all the appropriate control and monitoring systems are installed and working properly;
- complying with legal obligations;
- behavioural factors.

Thus, strategic management is concerned with the managerial decision-making process associated with the setting of objectives and the methods used to achieve those objectives in terms of policies, resource allocation, administration, operating and control systems and organizational structure.

Without strategic management the most likely outcome would be losses in time, money and talent. Where an organization is not being truly managed, problems would arise relating to rules, guidelines, yardsticks and resource allocation. Risk would be increased, and the quality of the managerial decisions would no doubt suffer.

CORPORATE STRATEGY AND OBJECTIVES

Corporate strategy relates to the means by which the corporate objectives are to be achieved. Corporate objectives are those which aim at the attainment of a desired future course for the company as a whole. They provide: *motivation, guidelines for action, values* for the conduct of the business, and a *basis for measuring performance*. If the objectives are to be of any use to management it is considered essential that they should be:

- quantifiable;
- achievable; and
- clearly ranked so as to indicate priorities.

However, all businesses have a multiplicity of objectives, many of which are non-economic, e.g. social objectives. Conflicts between objectives do arise and should be resolved. They can be:

- *Economic versus non-economic.*

- *Long-term versus short-term.* For example, not monitoring the environment could be disastrous in the long term.
- *Personal objectives versus company objectives.* This area needs to be watched most carefully, e.g. certain managers endeavour to create their own empires, the building of which could involve the company in heavy losses in the future.
- *State objectives versus multinational companies' objectives.* Conflicts may arise in areas of employment, location policy, transfer pricing, etc.

CORPORATE PLANNING

Corporate planning involves the complex process of systematically reviewing an organization's long-term future prospects (see Figure 15.1).

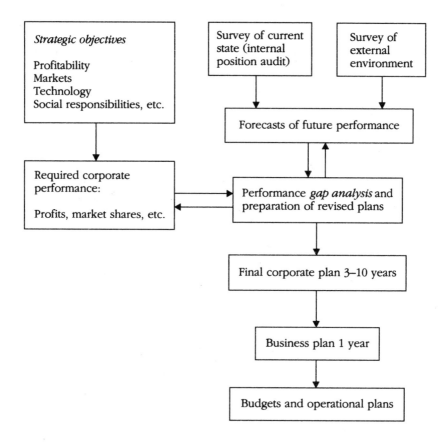

Figure 15.1 The corporate planning process

Source: Chadwick, L. and Pike, R. (1985) *Management and Control of Capital in Industry*, London: CIMA

The analysis should provide information from which it is possible to identify a gap. The gap between the objectives and the forecast could, for instance, indicate that the company must search for new products and/or new markets. If the gap cannot be closed then the company will have no alternative but to amend the objectives concerned. Corporate planning is also about the thinking process that precedes action and is directed towards the current decision-making process with an eye to the future. The various component parts of the corporate planning process are as follows:

The formulation of corporate objectives

This is the real starting point. If you fire an arrow at a target that just isn't there, you will never hit it! Objectives provide a target against which to compare performance and a sense of purpose and direction.

Assessing the complex and diverse environment in which the company operates

The essential elements of a system for planning and evaluting capital investments are illustrated in Figure 15.2, and are given on page 140.

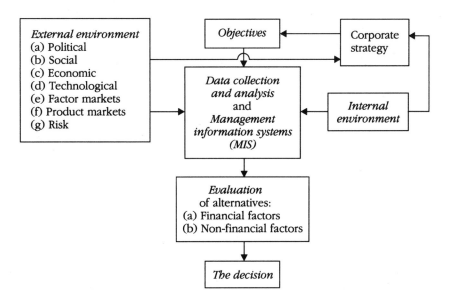

Figure 15.2 The capital investment decision

Source: Chadwick, L. and Pike, R. (1985) *Management and Control of Capital in Industry*, London: CIMA

- *Objectives.* All projects should be in line with the objectives and/or the policy of the company concerned. In particular, the company's objectives relating to the required return on capital employed should be clearly stated and understood.
- *Data collection and analysis.* Data has to be collected, classified, analysed and presented in a form appropriate to the needs and understanding of the user. A key decision that has to be made is the method(s) by which the investment is to be appraised, e.g. discounted cash flow.
- *The management information system.* The provision of relevant and appropriate information to management can most certainly enhance the decision-making process.

  An effective management information system is therefore a pre-requisite for efficient planning and control. The quality of the information will help to determine the accuracy of forecasts relating to future performance. However, it is possible to provide management with too much information, and information overload tends to weigh them down. The quality of the information rather than its quantity is therefore closely linked to the quality of the decision-making.
- *Monitoring the external environment.* The external environment in which a firm operates is diverse and complex. It must be continuously monitored to reveal threats and opportunities which could, at a stroke, change the whole nature of the firm's capital investment programme, e.g. political instability in the country of a major customer.
- *The internal environment.* A firm cannot ignore its own internal environment and analysis will indicate strengths and weaknesses, e.g. in industrial relations, idle capacity etc. The acceptance by workers of new plant or new processes can be of vital importance.
- *Evaluation.* In addition to the financial factors which have to be examined, management must also take various non-financial factors into account, e.g. availability of spare parts, flexibility, standardization etc.

A decision to go ahead with an investment does not end the story. The investment should be carefully monitored, and changes in the environment cannot be ignored. Companies must be able to adjust rapidly to meet enforced changes in circumstances if they are to survive and prosper. The real value of a business is the sum of the value of its existing assets plus the value of its future investment opportunities. Existing assets represent prior investment decisions, the consequences of which (in terms of profits and cash flows) are still with us. Future investment opportunities represent the scope a business possesses for making profitable investment decisions in the future. The investment potential will vary from firm to firm and industry to industry and will depend, to a large extent, on:

- management's ability to generate, select and execute investment projects;
- its capacity to raise funds to finance investments; and
- corporate strategy.

The importance of monitoring

Management must always be aware of the changes taking place at the interface between the company and its environment. It is therefore, essential that the environment is monitored on a regular basis, thus providing a continuous flow of relevant information. The monitoring should extend to areas such as the following:

Internal (internal position audit)

- the corporate objectives;
- the operation of all the functional areas;
- strengths, weaknesses, threats and opportunities.

External environment (at home and abroad)

- *Products*, e.g. performance, pricing, product lifecycles, packaging.
- *Product markets*, e.g. demand, competition.
- *Factor markets*, e.g. availability of raw materials, labour supply, finance.
- *The economic environment*, e.g. inflation, growth targets, taxation measures.
- *The technological environment*, e.g. new developments. It is also advisable to monitor what is happening in industries, other than one's own. The Swiss watch industry suffered greatly in the past because of the rapid developments in electronics.
- *The political environment*, e.g. monopolies, consumer protection, legislation.
- *The social environment*, e.g. noise, pollution, population structure, education.

Companies should be fully aware of their strengths and weaknesses and ready and able to respond to threats and opportunities that present themselves as a result of *monitoring* the environment, i.e. carrying out a SWOT analysis (see Figure 15.3).

DETERMINING THE CORPORATE STRATEGY

If you go on a journey without a map of the route, you are likely to get lost. The journey could also turn out to be long, hazardous and tiring, and you could

Strengths 'S'	Weaknesses 'W'
Opportunities 'O'	Threats 'T'

Figure 15.3 SWOT Analysis

end up going nowhere at all! Corporate strategy, in effect, provides a map: a map for the firm of the policy which has to be pursued to ensure that the company moves in the right direction and achieves its ultimate goal. This involves the design and preparation of programmes of *action*, for both the long and short term.

Corporate structure

Corporate structure refers to the organizational structure necessary for implementing strategic decisions, defining responsibilities and lines of authority. The structure should be designed to facilitate the flow of information to and from the decision-makers. The design should also ensure that adequate feedback channels are established and endeavour to foster co-ordination. Behavioural aspects should not be ignored as they affect the decision- making process within the corporate structure, for example, in the following ways.

- *Gate-keeping.* Gate-keeping is a name used to describe an employee who is in charge of an information junction. The gate-keeper may stop information passing through the information junction for a variety of reasons. They are in a position of power where they can exercise control over certain flows of information, and by their action can determine what management will and will not see.
- *Political access.* If you had the 'king's ear' in the middle ages you had political access. In industry and commerce political access is used to describe the individuals in an organization who have the ear of their top decision-makers: for example, the managing director. Access to them enables such individuals to maybe exert some influence upon the decision-making process.

The value of the corporate planning process arises directly from the careful consideration of corporate objectives, strengths, weaknesses, threats and opportunities. It does not produce a blueprint for the future, as it is impossible to forecast the future with accuracy. However, forecasting (e.g. long-term financial forecasting) is an essential part of the planning process. It should have built-in flexibility so as to enable the firm to change direction. It is not an attempt to eliminate risk but rather an attempt to enable management to understand the nature of risk. Corporate planning is not the making of future decisions. It is concerned with the process of making decisions **now** about the future, in terms of objectives and the means necessary to achieve those objectives.

Note

It should be noted that there are numerous and conflicting definitions of the terms, strategic management, corporate structure, corporate objectives, and corporate planning.

SUMMARY

Strategic management is concerned with the setting of corporate objectives and the formulation of the policy to achieve those objectives. It is concerned with the allocation of resources, company survival, the search for alternative courses of action, communicating, managing risk, performance evaluation, monitoring the environment, the organizational structure, systems evaluations, legal requirements and behavioural considerations.

If possible, objectives set should be *quantifiable, achievable* and *clearly ranked. Corporate planning* involves the systematic review and evaluation of a company/organization's future prospects, and the highlighting of gaps so as to be able to revise plans accordingly. It is most important that the *external and internal environments* are *monitored* on a frequent basis and subjected to close scrutiny by the company/organization. *Behavioural factors* cannot and should not be ignored. Their influences within the corporate structure can affect decision-making.

Self-assessments 15.1

When you have had a go at each of these self-assessments, compare your answer with the appropriate section of this chapter.

1 Explain briefly what strategic management seeks to do and how it does it.
2 Describe how the corporate planning process may take place.
3 Why is it so important for a company to monitor its internal and external environment and what does it have to monitor?
4 How can 'gate-keeping' and 'political access' affect a company's decision-making processes?
5 What is SWOT analysis and how can it help a business to survive and prosper?

Further reading

Ansoff, H.I. (1987) *Corporate Strategy*, London: Penguin.
Argenti, J. (1982) *Systematic Corporate Planning*, US: Van Nostrand Reinhold.
Chandler, A.D. (1962) *Strategy and Structure*, US: MIT Press.
Cyert, R. and March, J.G.A. (1992) *A Behavioural Theory of the Firm*, Oxford: Blackwell.
Steiner, G. (1969) *Top Management Planning*, US: Free Press.

Section VI

Other topics

Chapter 16

Reading the *Financial Times*

Objectives

The sole objective of this chapter is to introduce you to the FT (*Financial Times*) in terms of what it covers and how to read the data which is published on the London Share Service. The only real way of coming to terms with reading, and understanding the *Financial Times* is actually to buy one and read it! However, what is described here is an attempt to help you interpret it, and to give you an idea as to what you may find within its pages!

The *Financial Times*, the UK's leading business newspaper now regards itself as Europe's business newspaper too. This claim is fully supported by its contents. Much of the information which it publishes is about Europe and indeed the rest of the world. Taking a copy at random can give a good insight into exactly what is covered, the variety, the depth, the detailed statistics and the reports.

For illustration purposes, a copy was taken out at random and turned out to be a most interesting choice. The *Financial Times*, dated Tuesday 4 January 1994 was packed full of financial data. As with all newspapers its front page headlines introduced the leading stories which turned out to be:

Asia and Europe in buoyant mood as City returns to trading today. Markets worldwide enter new year with fresh gains.

[This article reported the surge in both European and Asian stock markets in contrast to a subdued market on Wall Street.]

Increase in taxes will not undermine recovery.

[This was based on a *Financial Times* survey of thirty-nine independent economic forecasters in which it was considered that tax increases in the spring were not expected to blow the UK's economic recovery off course.]

Review of media ownership may open foreign markets.

[This was about a wide-ranging government review of UK cross-media ownership designed to encourage British companies to take advantage of opportunities in the international media markets.]

J.P. Morgan differed with Bank of Spain over Banesto.

[This was a report about Banesto's (i.e. Banco Espanol de Credito) falling share price, assets being over-valued and the intervention by the Bank of Spain.]

Also highlighted on the front page were details of special features which were:

- Economic forecasts for 1994. 'Bright for Britain' but 'Clouds over the US'.
- 'The challengers. Europe's new faces of 1994', about forthcoming elections in member states.
- 'Put it on the card. How to save on calls from hotels.'

All of this was covered in the first section of the newspaper together with other international news, UK news, weather, letters, people, management, the arts, TV and radio etc.

The second section of the newspaper is headed 'Companies and Markets'. This section has various articles, reports, analyses, statistics and company information, e.g. markets this week, foreign exchanges, managed funds, money markets, recent issues, share information and world stock markets etc.

The leading stories were:

- 'A new way of dealing with risk': about revised US capital rules for investors.
- 'Investors upbeat on US retailing take over': about Federated Department Stores trying to take over Macys.
- 'French bank group in capital increase': a report about (CCF) Credit Commercial de France planning to increase its capital and take advantage of the buoyant state of affairs on the Paris stock exchange.

The front page of this second section, in addition to highlighting company news, also gave some details about the revised all-share classification taking effect from this issue, the first major overhaul in two decades.

Of particular interest to financial management were the statistics which are published and were:

> Base lending rates
> FT – World Indices
> FT – Guide to Currencies
> Foreign exchanges
> London recent issues
> London Share Service
> Money markets
> New international bond issues
> World stock market indices

The random selection of this issue was indeed quite fortunate, on pages 28 and 29 was published the new UK share classification. The classification lists each company and indicates the sector to which it belongs. For example:

Name of company with or without various symbols etc.	Price	W'k % change	Div net	Div cov	Dividends paid	Last ×d	City Line
Allied Leisure ♧N□	42		3.0	1.1	Dec. May	18.0	4643
Bass qN□	536 × d	– 2.7	19.8	1.9	Feb. Jul.	13.12	1772

Figure 16.1 Share Service pages of the *Financial Times*

Allied Leisure	Leisure & Hotels
Bass	Breweries
Glaxo	Pharmaceuticals
Hanson	Diversified Industrials
Rolls Royce	Engineering
Tie Rack	Retailers
Wickes	Building Materials & Merchants

The London Share Service pages provide information about share prices and dividends, etc, companies being listed alphabetically for each sector. The information is provided in the format shown in Figure 16.1.

There are a number of symbols which are used to provide the reader with additional information, e.g. □ is an indication of a stock which is most actively traded, ♣ means that a free annual/interim report is available, ♦ shows that a merger bid or re-organization is in progress.

The additional letters which are also sometimes shown with the symbols following the company name also provide the user with additional information, examples are:

a	=	annualized dividend
c	=	cents
g	=	assumed dividend
q	=	earnings based on preliminary figures
t	=	indicated dividend cover relates to previous dividend
L	=	estimated annualized dividend cover based on latest annual earnings
N	=	Figures based on IIMR 'Headline Earnings'
Q	=	Gross

This list is not complete but does provide you with an insight into the kind of messages they are trying to communicate. Abbreviations can also be found within the data generated, e.g. xd means ex dividend, xc denotes an ex scrip issue, and so on. A full list of the symbols and letters is published alongside the data in the *Financial Times*.

The other data which is shown consists of:

● *The price*. This is the closing mid-price of the shares stated in pence unless otherwise stated, e.g. Allied Leisure 42p and Bass 536pxd. Notice also, that the Bass price stated is the ex dividend price, i.e. the buyer will not receive the next dividend.

- The W'k % change is the weekly percentage change, in the case of Bass the shares have gone down by 2.7 per cent.
- Div net, is the net of tax dividend.
- Div Cov, is the dividend cover calculated by comparing the 'gross dividend' with the net profit after tax.
- City line. The FT Cityline provides up-to-the-second share prices by dialling the 4-digit code after the appropriate number given in the *Financial Times*.

SUMMARY

As you have observed, the *Financial Times* (FT) provides a lot of financial information by way of articles, reports, surveys, statistics etc. This makes it not just the leading business newspaper for the UK and Europe, but also a very important business newspaper for the world. One of its premier services is the data which it supplies re the London Share Service in which it gives details of share prices, their movements, dividends and various other data.

FINANCIAL TIMES PROJECTS/DISCUSSIONS

Obtain a copy/copies of the *Financial Times* and:

16.1 (a) Read a selection of articles which are of interest from a financial management point of view, and highlight the important points, and
(b) Discuss with others or make a presentation of your findings, critical comments etc.

16.2 Have a look at what is happening to the shares of companies in the London Share Service for a sector of your own choice. (You should also look up, via the key supplied in the FT any symbols, letters or abbreviations you do not know the meaning of.)

16.3 Look at eight companies of your choice in the London Share Service, two from each of four sectors, and follow their progress for a minimum of two weeks. Explain what has happened to the share price and dividends where movements have taken place. (This could also be done over a number of months, monitoring on, say, the Tuesday of each week or on some other day.)

Chapter 17

Mergers and takeovers

Objectives

When you have read this chapter you should be able to:

- state some of the reasons for takeovers and mergers;
- identify the stages in a takeover bid;
- formulate an offer for shares;
- identify procedures used as part of a defensive strategy.

INTRODUCTION

If one company holds more than 50 per cent of the voting shares in another company, it has control over it. The controlling company is called the parent company and the controlled company is its subsidiary. A group exists when there are two or more companies in the relationship of parent and subsidiary.

A merger is where the company acquired is merged into the existing group of companies, retaining its own identity. With a takeover the company acquired may be closed down. This may apply where a competitor is acquired with the express purpose of killing off the opposition.

REASONS FOR MERGERS

There are various reasons for mergers, including the following.

1 *Operating economies.*
    (a) vertical versus horizontal integration: the objective of vertical integration is to control the operations from production through to distribution. Thus a company without distribution facilities may acquire a company specializing in distribution. Horizontal integration is where two similar businesses merge;
    (b) elimination of duplicate facilities, such as marketing, purchasing, finance.
2 *Fiscal.* There could be tax advantages associated with the merger, such as the acquisition of a tax loss company.

3   *Diversification*. By diversifying, the business risk is spread.
4   *Growth*. The acquisition of a growth company by a company whose growth is declining.
5   *The acquisition of able management and know-how.*

Self-assessment 17.1

Distinguish between a merger and a takeover.

SELECTION OF THE TARGET COMPANY

Having decided to pursue a policy of acquisition by merger, the directors of the attacking company should produce a set of criteria, ranked in order of importance, against which the target company can be judged. Such criteria will usually include size, products, location, strengths of existing management and financial matters. Possible targets are then assessed against these pre-determined criteria and ranked accordingly. At this stage some possible targets may be rejected. The remainder require further research, using such public information as is available in order to arrive at eventual targets and the price to be paid for them.

Bidding strategy

The directors of the attacking company should always bear in mind that the purpose of the attack is to maximize the shareholder wealth of the attacking company. The bidding strategy should always have this in mind, and the directors should not succumb to bids based on prestige or other non-financial factors.

In formulating a bidding strategy the directors will need to take the following into account:

1   the composition of the shareholders of the defending company;
2   the price to pay, with a pre-determined maximum;
3   the package to offer;
4   the approach to the defending board of directors;
5   the action required if the bid is opposed.

The composition of the shareholders

The composition of the shareholders can be ascertained by becoming a shareholder of the defending company, in which case they will have the right of inspection of the register of members. Alternatively, the last published accounts may provide a suitable analysis of shareholders. The purpose is to find out who owns the company: private shareholders, institutions, family holdings. All these will give an insight into any resistance to the bid.

The bid price

The bid price will be considered in the light of any prevailing quoted share price on the stock market and share valuations based on net assets, earnings and dividends. The maximum bid price for the company is the discounted future income stream, but this will be difficult to determine. In order to gain acceptance by the shareholders of the defending company, the bid price would have to be in excess of the prevailing share price. In addition, if the share price on the stock market has fallen recently, shareholders who bought at a high level might be reluctant to sell at a price which will leave them showing a loss.

The package

The package to be offered will depend upon what the attacking company is able to offer. The offer might be in cash, debentures, convertible loan stock, preference shares, ordinary shares or a combination of any of these. If the attacking company is already highly geared it may not wish to increase its gearing level by bidding in debentures or convertibles. Alternatively, it may be short of cash and a bid in cash may create liquidity problems. The advantage of bidding in cash is that the value is constant throughout the period of negotiation and the value is quantified and readily understood by all participants. There could be capital gains tax implications for the recipient shareholder. By issuing shares or debentures, a capital gains tax is avoided as the existing shares have not been realized, merely exchanged. Ordinary shares would be acceptable with institutional investors looking for growth. The problem of issuing shares is that there can be variations in value through time viz.:

An offer of 3 shares at £1.20 for 2 at £1.80 equates in both cases to £3.60. If the shares of the defending company go up in value to say £2.00, then the attacking company would be forced to revise its bid as they would be offering only £3.60 for shares currently worth £4.00.

Self-assessment 17.2

The shares of A Plc and B Plc are currently valued at £1.25 and £0.75 respectively. How many shares should A Plc offer to match up exactly to the value of B Plc?

The approach to the board

The approach to the board of the defending company can in the first instance be informal and friendly, with a view to gaining their support. A meeting can be arranged and the details of the bid outlined. The bid price will be presented at this stage. If this is rejected it is usual to increase the offer. If necessary a third and final offer can be made.

The action required if the bid is opposed

If the bid is to be defended, the board of the defending company will circulate details of the reasons for the defence to its shareholders. If the attacking company is already a shareholder, their board of directors will be provided with invaluable information for use in the attempted takeover. This may lead to a revised offer or withdrawal from the bid.

Self-assessment 17.3

List four reasons for one company to merge with another.

Self-assessment 17.4

Urban Plc wishes to acquire the whole of the share capital of Rural Ltd, a private company engaged in the same trade as itself, through an exchange of securities.

The following information relates to each company:

Urban Plc
Current market price per share	£2.25
Dividend yield	7.5%
Earnings per share	£0.25
Price/earnings ratio	9

Rural Ltd
Net assets value per share	£4.30
Dividend per share	£0.30
Earnings per share	£0.50

You are required to:

1 calculate the value per share for Rural Ltd based upon dividends and earnings;
2 recommend the number of shares to be offered by Urban Plc for shares in Rural Ltd.

Defensive strategy

In formulating a defensive strategy, the board of directors of the defending company must protect the interests of their shareholders at all times. Before any enquiry is received, it is important for the board to maintain good relations with its shareholders and to protect the company's public image. This it can do by having regard to shareholder preferences and needs. The board should ensure that adverse trends do not develop and the share price is a fair reflection of its true value. Technical defences include making long-term contracts with key personnel, as these will act as a disincentive to an attacker. Gearing levels should be kept on the high side as low-geared companies are more attractive to an attacker than those with high gearing.

Once an enquiry has been received the price which would not be rejected should be calculated, bringing in all the favourable factors. All the worst features of the company are disclosed to the attacker in the hope that they will be deterred. At this stage the attacker is scrutinized for any weakness which could be used in the defence. Delaying tactics are often adopted in order to gain time.

After the bid is made to the shareholders the board of the defending company must give a convincing reason for rejecting the offer. This may simply be that the price is too low. This is often used as a defence where the offer is in cash or debentures. If shares are offered, the record of the management of the attacking company is the subject of criticism. To support their arguments, the board of the defending company will often produce favourable profit forecasts and a revalued balance sheet with the intention of forcing up their own share price. All this is with a view to making the price too high for the attacker, or at least to force them to make another offer at a higher price.

Self-assessment 17.5

List six elements that may comprise part of a defensive strategy.

SUMMARY

In this chapter you have been introduced to the complex subject of mergers and takeovers. The reasons why mergers take place have been considered. The selection of possible targets and the procedures adopted by attacking and defending companies have been discussed. Finally, the calculation of the terms of the offer, linking in with the studies on share valuation have been explained.

Further reading

Brealey, R. and Myers, S. (1991) *Principles of Corporate Finance*, London: McGraw Hill.
Weston, J.F. and Copeland, T.E. (1988) *Managerial Finance*, London: Cassell.

Chapter 18

Introduction to foreign exchange management

This chapter introduces you to what is a very wide and specialized subject area. Its sole aim is to provide you with a brief appreciation of the risk faced and some of the ways in which management may approach it.

Objectives

When you have read this chapter you should be in a position to:

- appreciate the dangers of currency fluctuations;
- describe the ways in which management may attempt to prevent or reduce the risk, in particular via hedging and foreign currency swaps.

Two of the terms which are used in this chapter may be unfamiliar. They are:

- *Spot rate.* The currency rate for immediate delivery of currency.
- *Forward rate.* The currency rate quoted now for delivery at some future specified date, e.g. in 3 months' time.

The principal aim of foreign exchange management, is to conduct the financial affairs of a business/organization in a way which will help to prevent or minimize losses caused by fluctuating currency values. This is a risk which all businesses which engage in exporting and/or importing must face.

The exchange rate has been described by Blommaert *et al.* in their *Financial Decision Making* text as:

A ratio of the monetary units of one country's currency divided by the number of economically equivalent monetary units of another country.

Management need to appreciate how foreign currency transactions are accounted for and their impact upon their company/organization. Poor management of foreign currency could not just lose a lot of money but could endanger the company/organization's very survival.

In the example illustrated, Figure 18.1, company X in the UK has reduced the risk of currency fluctuations by invoicing in their own currency. This places the exchange risk on to company Y who have to pay in sterling at some future

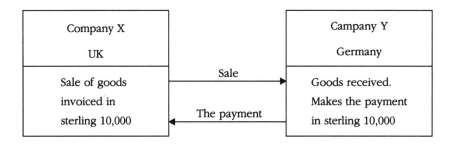

Figure 18.1 Invoicing in your own currency

date. It also means that company Y has to deal with the accounting implications in its accounting books/records. It must be noted that in the absence of any currency hedging by the German company, company Y, both companies could win or lose out, as explained below.

If at the date of the sale the rate of exchange was 2.5 DM to the £, the value of the sale in DM would be 25,000 DM. If when the payment was made the exchange rate was 2.35 DM to the £, the value of the sale in DM would be 23,500 DM. This would benefit the German company which would, in effect, have had to pay 23,500 DM for goods valued at the date of sale at 25,000 DM. If the UK company has invoiced at 25,000 DM, the payment they would have received at the exchange rate of 2.35 DM would have been £10,638.30p! However, the illustration could also be vice versa. Either way the UK company does receive the full sterling value invoice price because it has invoiced in sterling.

In Figure 18.2, company X, the seller, has to face the risk of fluctuations in the franc. For illustration purposes, we will assume that at the date of the sale the exchange rate was 8.3 francs to the pound sterling, and that when payment was received the rate of exchange was 8.75 F.

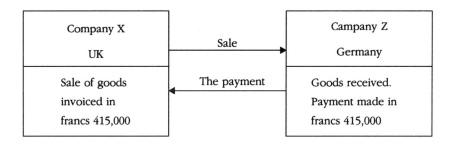

Figure 18.2 Invoicing in your customer's currency

Value in sterling at the date of the sale:

$$\frac{415,000\,\text{F}}{8.3} = £50,000$$

Value in sterling at the date of receiving the payment from France:

$$\frac{415,000\,\text{F}}{8.75} = £47,428.57\text{p}$$

It can be observed from a review of the figures that company X, in the absence of any hedging will lose £2,571.43p because of the change in the exchange rate. Company X, would also have to deal with the accounting recording aspects of the currency transaction in its book and records. Note that if we were dealing with bigger numbers, e.g. sales of £500,000, the profits/losses from transaction in foreign currency could be quite considerable!

If in the examples illustrated in Figure 19.1 and 19.2 the positions were reversed, and company X was the buyer, it would have the greatest exchange risk where it was paying for the goods received in the currency of the vendor.

GUARDING AGAINST THE RISK OF FOREIGN CURRENCY FLUCTUATIONS

Movements in the relative values of national currencies have played havoc with, and complicated international business transactions. There are, however, a number of ways in which management can attempt to prevent and minimize losses caused by changing currency values. Some of these are as follows:

Hedging

Hedging is a method by which a risk in one direction can be offset by a risk in another direction which tends to compensate and cancel out the risk. For example, if you have to pay an overseas supplier for goods invoiced at 180,000 Dutch guilders in 3 months' time, you could buy the 180,000 Dutch guilders on the *forward foreign exchange market* now. Whatever happens to the Dutch guilder in 3 months' time would then cease to matter. The 180,000 Dutch guilders purchased could be held in a bank and be earning some interest up to the date on which payment has to be made. Hedging has been made necessary because of the unpredictability of the future and the instability of international money markets.

Pre-payment of imports

If legislation permits, it may be possible to pre-pay imports and thereby eliminate any future risk.

Foreign currency swap

Making use of a foreign currency swap may happen where two parties agree to exchange one currency for another and then after a specified period of time return the same amount of currencies to their original owner. It is defined by Eiteman *et al.* as:

> a simultaneous spot-and-forward transaction in the foreign exchange market, with the forward transaction reversing the spot transaction.

Thus, a parent company which wishes to loan funds to its overseas subsidiary and do away with the exchange risk can:

1 Buy the necessary foreign exchange in the 'spot market'.
2 At the same time buy the home currency for forward delivery against the foreign exchange which will be repaid by the subsidiary on the date specified.
● Do some compensatory inter-company setting off of international debts via debits and credits within the recording system, i.e. to cancel out inter-company indebtedness.
● If legislation permits, keep certain bank accounts in the currencies which tend to be used a lot, so that payments/receipts/transfers to other accounts can be made as and when necessary.
● Taking out a foreign currency loan. There are various scenarios which the company taking out the loan can then consider.
● In the UK, make use of the services provided by ECGD (Export Credits Guarantee Department).

SUMMARY

Foreign exchange management concerns itself with the elimination and/or reduction of risk which may be caused by fluctuations in foreign currencies. A business may send or receive an invoice which is denominated in their own currency or a foreign currency. Those invoices for sales or purchases which are denominated in the foreign currency expose them to foreign exchange risks. Management can employ quite a large number of measures to help them prevent or reduce the risk of making a foreign currency loss. Some of the measures which were reviewed here, were:

● hedging via the forward foreign exchange market;
● the prepayment of imports;
● foreign currency swaps;
● compensating debits and credits;
● keeping certain bank accounts in the foreign currencies which are used;
● using loans taken out in foreign currencies;
● taking advantage of the services available in the UK from ECGD.

Self-assessments 18.1

When you have attempted these, compare your answer with the appropriate sections of this chapter.

1 Explain briefly the foreign currency risks which may be applicable to the international buyers and the sellers of certain products.
2 How can management attempt to prevent or reduce a foreign currency loss?

Further reading

Blommaert, A.M.M., Blommaert, J.M.J. and Hayes, R.S. (1991) *Financial Decision Making*, London: Prentice Hall.

Buckley, A. (1990) *The Essence of International Money*, London: Prentice Hall.

Copeland, L.S. (1994) *Exchange Rates and International Finance*, Wokingham: Addison-Wesley.

Eiteman, D.K., Stonehill, A.I. and Moffett, M.H. (1995) *Multinational Business Finance*, 7th edn, Wokingham: Addison-Wesley.

Pike, R. and Neale, B. (1993) *Corporate Finance and Investment*, London: Prentice Hall.

The UK business taxation system

Many financial management texts use illustrations and look at theories which assume a world without taxes. In the real world however, we do have taxes, and this is particularly true of the UK. Various taxes may be paid when goods are traded, dividends are paid, capital gains are made and when profits are generated. It is a fact of life that taxation does affect:

- cash flows;
- retained earnings;
- dividends paid out;
- the cost of certain fixed assets;
- decision making.

The tax factor could well be the make or break reason as to whether or not a particular project goes ahead.

THE TAX ON BUSINESS PROFITS

In arriving at the tax payable on the profits of a small business or a limited company, the profit as computed in the profit and loss account is *not* usually the figure on which the tax is calculated. Many accounting texts leave the reader with the impression that UK tax is calculated on the net profit before tax figure. This is *not* the case, a tax computation has to be prepared and eventual agreement reached with HM Inspector of Taxes on the actual figure which will have to be paid.

How is tax calculated?

A typical UK tax computation will be drafted along the following lines:

1 It starts with the net profit before tax figure.
2 Depreciation which has been deducted in computing the net profit before tax is then added back. The reason for this is that there are special tax allowances which have to be used in place of depreciation, called *capital allowances* (see 'Capital allowances', later on in this appendix).

3   Any losses on the sale of fixed assets are added back
4   Any profits on the sale of fixed assets are deducted
5   The outcome of items 1–4 above will then represent the net profit before tax, depreciation and profits or losses on the sale of fixed assets.
6   Expenditure, charged in the profit and loss account but which is not an allowable deduction for tax purposes has to be added back. Examples of expenditure which is not allowed as a deduction for tax purposes are:
   ● for small businesses, private personal expenditure, e.g. rent etc. for own living accommodation, drawings of cash/assets for personal use;
   ● for all businesses/companies, amounts paid out on income tax, corporation tax, capital gains etc, or for penalties for breaking the law, e.g. motoring fines;
   ● the cost of improvements to property
   The main criteria is that to be allowed as an expense for tax purposes, the expense must have been paid out *wholly and exclusively for the purposes of the business*. Thus, expenses such as actual bad debts, interest on business loans, business insurance, the rent and repair of business premises etc. are all allowable.
7   Any receipts which are not taxable, possibly because they have been taxed already or are to be taxed under a different tax schedule, must be deducted in computing the taxable profit (or loss).
8   Capital allowances are computed and deducted in computing the net assessment.
9   For companies, other more complex tax matters have to be dealt with, e.g. the treatment of the ACT (advance corporation tax) and the tax matters relating to investment income and capital gains etc.
10   Agreement has to be reached with HM Inspector of Taxes and an assessment raised.

WHEN IS THE TAX DUE TO BE PAID?

A non-company

For non-companies, businesses and professions, they are taxed under schedule D cases I and II. Their year of assessment runs from 6 April to the following 5 April, and except for special provisions which relate to commencement, cessation and the change of accounting date, they are assessed on '*a preceding year basis*'. For example:

A business which makes up its accounts to 31 December, would be assessed:

Year end	year of assessment
31 December 19X4	19X5/X6
31 December 19X5	19X6/X7

The year 31 December 19X4 ends within the actual tax year 19X4/X5, and so forms the basis period of assessment for the next tax year 19X5/X6. The tax payable under schedule D I and II is *income tax* and payable in two instalments:

- The first instalment on 1 January *within* the year of assessment, e.g. for 19X5/X6, this would be 1 January 19X6.
- The second instalment on the 1 July following the year of assessment, e.g. for 19X5/X6, this would be 1 July 19X6.

The rates of income tax do fluctuate and the rates paid will depend upon the income and tax allowances of the individual/s who own the business. There may be a lower rate band, e.g. 20 per cent, a basic rate band 25 per cent and one or more higher rate bands. It is dangerous here to be too specific, as rates can and do change from time to time.

Companies

The profits, gains and income of companies is taxed via *corporation tax*, in most cases by reference to the company's usual accounting period. Where a change in the rate of corporation tax takes place and the company's year end does not correspond with the corporation tax 'financial year', it will be necessary to apportion that company's results on a time basis and charge them at the appropriate rates. The rates at which corporation tax is charged are fixed for the corporation tax year, simply called '*the financial year*' which runs from 1 April to the following 31 March. Here also, rates do change from time to time. In recent years they have tended to hover around the 33 per cent mark with lower rates of around 25 per cent for small companies, although in times gone by, there were much higher rates, e.g. 52 per cent!

- Currently, corporation tax is due to be payed nine months after the company's year end to which it relates. Failure to pay corporation tax by the due date will attract an interest charge from that date.

CAPITAL ALLOWANCES

Plant, machinery, equipment and motor vehicles

Although capital allowances have been described as 'being given in lieu of depreciation', they have over the years been used by governments as a device to stimulate investment. The allowances which have been used, some of which are still in use are as follows:

- *An investment allowance, first year allowance (initial allowance).* This type of allowance is a one off allowance which may or may not be deducted in computing the assets written down value.

● *A writing down allowance.* This could either be given from year 1 or from year 2 in cases where the first year allowance etc were given in year 1.

The following brief examples illustrate how they work or could work:

Example 1: An investment allowance

	£
Plant cost: year 1	250,000
Investment allowance (40%)	100,000 (not deducted from cost)

Year 2: £250,000 attracting allowances at 25 per cent each year on a reducing balance method.

Example 2: A first year allowance

	£
Machinery cost: year 1	120,000
Less: first year allowance @ 30%	36,000
Written down value (WDV)	84,000
Year 2: writing down allowance @ 25%	21,000
Written down value (WDV)	63,000

Example 3: Just a writing down allowance each year

	£
Equipment cost: year 1	96,000
Less: writing down allowance @ 25%	24,000
Written down value (WDV)	72,000
Year 2: writing down allowance @ 25%	18,000
Written down value	54,000

The tax saving on all the above allowances is computed by multiplying the writing down allowance by the rate of tax applicable. For example, if the rate of tax was 35 per cent for year 1, for the £96,000 equipment in example 3, the tax benefit for year 1 would be the writing down allowance of £24,000 multiplied by 35 per cent = £8,400.

In addition to the rates of tax, and rates of capital allowances changing, it is not unheard of for the principles to change! Capital allowances simply have to be calculated according to the rules and rates applicable at the time.

Special rates and provisions do tend to apply to cars and vehicles capable of private use, e.g. if first year allowances higher than 25 per cent are given for plant, machinery, equipment, vans, lorries, etc., they may not apply to cars. In that case cars may just have a 25 per cent rate applied on the reducing balance basis from year 1 onwards.

If a fixed asset on which capital allowances have been claimed is sold, the profit or loss on sale is termed *a balancing charge* or *balancing allowance* respectively, and is computed as follows.

Assuming that the equipment written down to £54,000 in year 2 (Example 3) was sold for £61,250.

Year 3	£
Sale proceeds	61,250
Less: Written down value b/f	54,000 (WDV)
Balancing charge	£7,250

If it had been sold for less than its WDV, there would be a balancing allowance. This follows the tax principle of charging tax on profits and providing tax relief for losses.

Industrial buildings

Capital allowances have been and still are available for expenditure which has been paid out for the construction of industrial buildings. The allowances which have tended to be used are as follows:

- an initial allowance, e.g. between 20 per cent and 100 per cent;
- a writing down allowance from the first year in which the building came into use, e.g. at the rate of 4 per cent.

The granting of such allowances could also be affected by government policy towards designated development areas and the small business sector, e.g. special rates for small industrial workshops.

CAPITAL GAINS TAX

As with other taxes, UK capital gains has also been subjected to a number of amendments since its introduction in 1965. The most significant amendment concerns disposals taking place after 5 April 1988. This changed the way in which the gain or loss is calculated and also reformed how the tax payable is calculated. Capital gains is payable when certain assets such as shares, land, buildings, and unit trust holdings etc. are disposed of (subject to an annual exemption limit for individuals; no exemption limit for companies).

Areas of particular interest to businesses/companies are:

- the disposal of a business;
- retirement relief relating to the disposal of business assets;
- the disposal of shares;
- roll-over relief, a situation in which a gain can be set off against a replacement asset;
- the indexation allowance, which helps overcome having gains created by inflation being taxed as a capital gain;
- offsetting business losses against capital gains.

The rate of tax payable by an individual will depend upon their highest rate tax band. Companies are liable to capital gains at the rate of corporation tax which is applicable to them, e.g. for a small company at the small companies rate.

VAT (VALUE ADDED TAX)

Those who are registered have to account for the tax, on a quarterly basis, unless they have been able, as in certain cases to account for it on a monthly basis. The tax payable (if any), or re-payable is calculated as follows:

Output tax (value added tax on sales)

Less: *Input tax* (value added tax on purchases, and business expenses relating to businesses/companies registered for VAT)

One or two points worthy of note and which you may find interesting are:

- the reported turnover figure (i.e. sales) in the profit and loss account should be shown net of VAT. Any VAT owing to the Customs & Excise at the end of the accounting period should be shown as a creditor in the balance sheet.
- VAT on certain fixed assets purchased which cannot be offset against the output tax, should be added to the cost of the asset. The cost of the asset plus the irrecoverable VAT is the figure on which any taxation capital allowances can be claimed.

Other areas of importance to businesses are the provisions relating to bad debts, exemptions, zero rating and the various special schemes, e.g. the tour operators' margin scheme, retailers, farmers etc.

OTHER AREAS

There are several other areas which may be of interest to businesses. They are:

- personal taxation matters for individuals and partnerships;
- the business expansion scheme (BES);
- income from property;
- inheritance tax;
- pensions.

CONCLUSION

The principles do not change all that often but the rates of tax and allowances do!

Further reading

A very useful and concise book about taxation is the relatively inexpensive *Daily Mail Income Tax Guide* which is published every year.

Appendix 2

Financial numeracy

INTRODUCTION

This appendix is intended to help readers who feel less comfortable with some of the financial calculations encountered in a text on financial management.

Simple interest

Self-assessment A.1

(a) How much will an investor have in 5 years' time if the initial investment is £1,300 and the simple rate of interest is 6 per cent per annum?
(b) A sum of £4,000 is borrowed for 3 years at a simple rate of interest of 7 per cent with no repayments during that period. What will be the amount of the total interest payable and the total amount paid?
(c) What sum was initially invested for 4 years at a simple rate of interest of 5 per cent if the final amount was £1,080?

Compound interest

Self-assessment A.2

(a) What would the answer be in 1(a) above if the compound rate of interest is used?
(b) What would the answer be in 1(b) above if the compound rate of interest is 6 per cent per annum?
(c) What sum was initially invested for 4 years at a compound rate of interest of 5 per cent if the final amount was £1,489?

Sinking funds

A sum of money (a fund) that is built up by setting aside cash for future use is called a sinking fund.

Self-assessment A.3

(a) You are planning to buy a new car 3 years from now and can set aside £2,000 now and at the start of each year. How much will you have set aside for the purchase if the annual interest rate is 8 per cent?

(b) How much would you have for the purchase if you saved for 4 years at £1,500 each year with an the annual rate of interest of 7 per cent?

Discounted cash flow

Self-assessment A.4

(a) Equipment is expected to be replaced in 2 years' time at a cost of £25,000. If the annual interest rate is 10 per cent, how much should be set aside now in order to meet the cost of the equipment.

(b) You are planning to buy a new car 3 years from now. You estimate the cost to be £12,000. How much will you have set aside now to meet the cost of the purchase if the annual interest rate is 8 per cent?

Annuities

Where amounts are received on a regular (annual) recurring basis, in return for the initial investment of a one-off payment.

Self-assessment A.5

(a) Would you accept an annuity which offered £1,375 at the end of each year, for 5 years, if the interest rate is 10 per cent and the initial investment required was £6,000?

(b) What would be the minimum amount of the annuity you would require?

Appendix 3

Present value discount tables

PRESENT VALUE OF £1

Year	5%	6%	7%	8%	9%	10%	11%	12%	13%	14%	15%	16%	17%	18%	19%	20%	21%	22%	23%	24%	25%	26%	27%	28%	29%	30%	35%	40%
0	1.000	1.000	1.000	1.000	1.000	1.000	1.000	1.000	1.000	1.000	1.000	1.000	1.000	1.000	1.000	1.000	1.000	1.000	1.000	1.000	1.000	1.000	1.000	1.000	1.000	1.000	1.000	1.000
1	.952	.943	.935	.926	.917	.909	.901	.893	.885	.877	.870	.862	.855	.847	.840	.833	.826	.820	.813	.807	.800	.794	.787	.781	.775	.769	.741	.714
2	.907	.890	.873	.857	.842	.826	.812	.797	.783	.769	.756	.743	.731	.718	.706	.694	.683	.672	.661	.650	.640	.630	.620	.610	.601	.592	.549	.510
3	.864	.840	.816	.794	.772	.751	.731	.712	.693	.675	.658	.641	.624	.609	.593	.579	.564	.551	.537	.524	.512	.500	.488	.477	.466	.455	.406	.364
4	.823	.792	.763	.735	.708	.683	.659	.636	.613	.592	.572	.552	.534	.516	.499	.482	.467	.451	.437	.423	.410	.397	.384	.373	.361	.350	.301	.260
5	.784	.747	.713	.681	.650	.621	.593	.567	.543	.519	.497	.476	.456	.437	.419	.402	.386	.370	.355	.341	.328	.315	.303	.291	.280	.269	.223	.186
6	.746	.705	.666	.630	.596	.564	.535	.507	.480	.456	.432	.410	.390	.370	.352	.335	.319	.303	.289	.275	.262	.250	.238	.227	.217	.207	.165	.133
7	.711	.665	.623	.583	.547	.513	.482	.452	.425	.400	.376	.354	.333	.314	.296	.279	.263	.249	.235	.222	.210	.198	.188	.178	.168	.159	.122	.095
8	.677	.627	.582	.540	.502	.467	.434	.404	.376	.351	.327	.305	.285	.266	.249	.233	.218	.204	.191	.179	.168	.157	.148	.139	.130	.123	.091	.068
9	.645	.592	.544	.500	.460	.424	.391	.361	.333	.308	.284	.263	.243	.225	.209	.194	.180	.167	.155	.144	.134	.125	.116	.108	.101	.094	.067	.048
10	.614	.558	.508	.463	.422	.386	.352	.322	.295	.270	.247	.227	.208	.191	.176	.162	.149	.137	.126	.116	.107	.099	.092	.085	.078	.073	.050	.035
11	.585	.527	.475	.429	.388	.350	.317	.287	.261	.237	.215	.195	.178	.162	.148	.135	.123	.112	.103	.094	.086	.079	.072	.066	.061	.056	.037	.025
12	.557	.497	.444	.397	.356	.319	.286	.257	.231	.208	.187	.168	.152	.137	.124	.112	.102	.092	.083	.076	.069	.062	.057	.052	.047	.043	.027	.018
13	.530	.469	.415	.368	.326	.290	.258	.229	.204	.182	.163	.145	.130	.116	.104	.093	.084	.075	.068	.061	.055	.050	.045	.040	.037	.033	.020	.013
14	.505	.442	.388	.340	.299	.263	.232	.205	.181	.160	.141	.125	.111	.099	.088	.078	.069	.062	.055	.049	.044	.039	.035	.032	.028	.025	.015	.009
15	.481	.417	.362	.315	.275	.239	.209	.183	.160	.140	.123	.108	.095	.084	.074	.065	.057	.051	.045	.040	.035	.031	.028	.025	.022	.020	.011	.006
16	.458	.394	.339	.292	.252	.218	.188	.163	.141	.123	.107	.093	.081	.071	.062	.054	.047	.042	.036	.032	.028	.025	.022	.019	.017	.015	.008	.005
17	.436	.371	.317	.270	.231	.198	.170	.146	.125	.108	.093	.080	.069	.060	.052	.045	.039	.034	.030	.026	.023	.020	.017	.015	.013	.012	.006	.003
18	.416	.350	.296	.250	.212	.180	.153	.130	.111	.095	.081	.069	.059	.051	.044	.038	.032	.028	.024	.021	.018	.016	.014	.012	.010	.009	.005	.002
19	.396	.331	.277	.232	.194	.164	.138	.116	.098	.083	.070	.060	.051	.043	.037	.031	.027	.023	.020	.017	.014	.012	.011	.009	.008	.007	.003	.002
20	.377	.312	.258	.215	.178	.149	.124	.104	.087	.073	.061	.051	.043	.037	.031	.026	.022	.019	.016	.014	.012	.010	.008	.007	.006	.005	.002	.001
25	.295	.233	.184	.146	.116	.092	.074	.059	.047	.038	.030	.025	.020	.016	.013	.011	.009	.007	.006	.005	.004	.003	.003	.002	.002	.001	.001	.000
30	.231	.174	.131	.099	.075	.057	.044	.033	.026	.020	.015	.012	.009	.007	.005	.004	.003	.003	.002	.002	.001	.001	.001	.001	.000	.000	.000	.000
35	.181	.130	.094	.068	.049	.036	.026	.019	.014	.010	.008	.006	.004	.003	.002	.002	.001	.001	.001	.001	.000	.000	.000	.000	.000	.000	.000	.000
40	.142	.097	.067	.046	.032	.022	.015	.011	.008	.005	.004	.003	.002	.001	.001	.001	.001	.000	.000	.000	.000	.000	.000	.000	.000	.000	.000	.000
45	.111	.073	.048	.031	.021	.014	.009	.006	.004	.003	.002	.001	.001	.001	.000	.000	.000	.000	.000	.000	.000	.000	.000	.000	.000	.000	.000	.000
50	.087	.054	.034	.021	.013	.009	.005	.003	.002	.001	.001	.001	.000	.000	.000	.000	.000	.000	.000	.000	.000	.000	.000	.000	.000	.000	.000	.000

Note: The above present value factors are based on year-end interest calculations

CUMULATIVE PRESENT VALUE OF £1 PER ANNUM
(i.e. present value of an annuity of £1)

Year	5%	6%	7%	8%	9%	10%	11%	12%	13%	14%	15%	16%	17%	18%	19%	20%	21%	22%	23%	24%	25%	26%	27%	28%	29%	30%	35%	40%
1	.952	.943	.935	.926	.917	.909	.901	.893	.885	.877	.870	.862	.855	.847	.840	.833	.826	.820	.813	.807	.800	.794	.787	.781	.775	.769	.741	.714
2	1.859	1.833	1.808	1.783	1.759	1.736	1.713	1.690	1.668	1.647	1.626	1.605	1.585	1.566	1.546	1.528	1.510	1.492	1.474	1.457	1.440	1.424	1.407	1.392	1.376	1.361	1.289	1.224
3	2.723	2.673	2.624	2.577	2.531	2.487	2.444	2.402	2.361	2.322	2.283	2.246	2.210	2.174	2.140	2.106	2.074	2.042	2.011	1.981	1.952	1.923	1.896	1.868	1.842	1.816	1.696	1.589
4	3.546	3.465	3.387	3.312	3.240	3.170	3.102	3.037	2.974	2.914	2.855	2.798	2.743	2.690	2.639	2.589	2.540	2.494	2.448	2.404	2.362	2.320	2.280	2.241	2.203	2.166	1.997	1.849
5	4.329	4.212	4.100	3.993	3.890	3.791	3.696	3.605	3.517	3.433	3.352	3.274	3.199	3.127	3.058	2.991	2.926	2.864	2.804	2.745	2.689	2.635	2.583	2.532	2.483	2.436	2.220	2.035
6	5.076	4.917	4.767	4.623	4.486	4.355	4.231	4.111	3.998	3.889	3.784	3.685	3.589	3.498	3.410	3.326	3.245	3.167	3.092	3.021	2.951	2.885	2.821	2.759	2.700	2.643	2.385	2.168
7	5.786	5.582	5.389	5.206	5.033	4.868	4.712	4.564	4.423	4.288	4.160	4.039	3.922	3.812	3.706	3.605	3.508	3.416	3.327	3.242	3.161	3.083	3.009	2.937	2.868	2.802	2.508	2.263
8	6.463	6.210	5.971	5.747	5.535	5.335	5.146	4.968	4.799	4.639	4.487	4.344	4.207	4.078	3.954	3.837	3.726	3.619	3.518	3.421	3.329	3.241	3.156	3.076	2.999	2.925	2.598	2.331
9	7.108	6.802	6.515	6.247	5.995	5.759	5.537	5.328	5.132	4.946	4.772	4.607	4.451	4.303	4.163	4.031	3.905	3.786	3.673	3.566	3.463	3.366	3.273	3.184	3.100	3.019	2.665	2.379
10	7.722	7.360	7.024	6.710	6.418	6.145	5.889	5.650	5.426	5.216	5.019	4.833	4.659	4.494	4.339	4.192	4.054	3.923	3.799	3.682	3.571	3.465	3.366	3.269	3.178	3.092	2.715	2.414
11	8.306	7.887	7.499	7.139	6.805	6.495	6.207	5.938	5.687	5.453	5.234	5.029	4.836	4.656	4.486	4.327	4.177	4.035	3.902	3.776	3.656	3.544	3.437	3.335	3.239	3.147	2.752	2.438
12	8.863	8.384	7.943	7.536	7.161	6.814	6.492	6.194	5.918	5.660	5.421	5.197	4.988	4.793	4.610	4.439	4.278	4.127	3.985	3.851	3.725	3.606	3.493	3.387	3.286	3.190	2.779	2.456
13	9.394	8.853	8.358	7.904	7.487	7.103	6.750	6.424	6.122	5.842	5.583	5.342	5.118	4.910	4.715	4.533	4.362	4.203	4.053	3.912	3.780	3.656	3.538	3.427	3.322	3.223	2.799	2.469
14	9.899	9.295	8.745	8.244	7.786	7.367	6.982	6.628	6.302	6.002	5.724	5.468	5.229	5.008	4.802	4.611	4.432	4.265	4.108	3.962	3.824	3.695	3.573	3.459	3.351	3.249	2.814	2.478
15	10.380	9.712	9.108	8.559	8.061	7.606	7.191	6.811	6.462	6.142	5.847	5.575	5.324	5.092	4.876	4.675	4.490	4.315	4.153	4.001	3.859	3.726	3.601	3.483	3.373	3.268	2.825	2.484
16	10.838	10.106	9.447	8.851	8.313	7.824	7.379	6.974	6.604	6.265	5.954	5.669	5.405	5.162	4.938	4.730	4.536	4.357	4.190	4.033	3.887	3.751	3.623	3.503	3.390	3.283	2.834	2.489
17	11.274	10.477	9.763	9.122	8.544	8.022	7.549	7.120	6.729	6.373	6.047	5.749	5.475	5.222	4.990	4.775	4.576	4.391	4.219	4.059	3.910	3.771	3.640	3.518	3.403	3.295	2.840	2.492
18	11.690	10.828	10.059	9.372	8.756	8.201	7.702	7.250	6.840	6.467	6.128	5.818	5.534	5.273	5.033	4.812	4.608	4.419	4.243	4.080	3.928	3.786	3.654	3.529	3.413	3.304	2.844	2.494
19	12.085	11.158	10.336	9.604	8.950	8.365	7.839	7.366	6.938	6.550	6.198	5.877	5.584	5.316	5.070	4.844	4.635	4.442	4.263	4.097	3.942	3.799	3.666	3.539	3.421	3.311	2.848	2.496
20	12.462	11.470	10.594	9.818	9.129	8.514	7.963	7.469	7.025	6.623	6.259	5.929	5.628	5.353	5.101	4.870	4.657	4.460	4.279	4.110	3.954	3.808	3.673	3.546	3.427	3.316	2.850	2.497
25	14.094	12.783	11.654	10.675	9.823	9.077	8.422	7.843	7.330	6.873	6.464	6.097	5.766	5.467	5.195	4.948	4.721	4.514	4.323	4.147	3.985	3.834	3.694	3.564	3.442	3.329	2.856	2.499
30	15.372	13.765	12.409	11.258	10.274	9.427	8.694	8.055	7.496	7.003	6.566	6.177	5.829	5.517	5.235	4.979	4.746	4.534	4.339	4.160	3.995	3.842	3.701	3.569	3.447	3.332	2.857	2.500
35	16.374	14.498	12.948	11.655	10.567	9.644	8.855	8.176	7.586	7.070	6.617	6.215	5.858	5.539	5.251	4.992	4.756	4.541	4.345	4.164	3.998	3.845	3.703	3.571	3.448	3.333	2.857	2.500
40	17.159	15.046	13.332	11.925	10.757	9.779	8.951	8.244	7.634	7.105	6.642	6.234	5.871	5.548	5.258	4.997	4.760	4.544	4.347	4.166	3.999	3.846	3.703	3.571	3.448	3.333	2.857	2.500
45	17.774	15.456	13.606	12.108	10.881	9.863	9.008	8.283	7.661	7.123	6.654	6.242	5.877	5.552	5.261	4.999	4.761	4.545	4.347	4.166	4.000	3.846	3.704	3.571	3.448	3.333	2.857	2.500
50	18.256	15.762	13.801	12.234	10.962	9.915	9.042	8.305	7.675	7.133	6.661	6.246	5.880	5.554	5.262	5.000	4.762	4.545	4.348	4.167	4.000	3.846	3.704	3.571	3.448	3.333	2.857	2.500

Note: The above present value factors are based on year-end interest calculations

Appendix 4

Suggested answers for self-assessments

THE FLOW OF FUNDS

1.1 Henry Ltd

Funds statement

Sources	£000s	
Net profit	4	
Decrease in stocks	10	
Increase in creditors	2	16
Uses		
Purchase of fixed assets	10	
Increase in debtors	4	14
Increase in cash/bank		2

1.2

Depreciation is a non-cash flow item and is neither a source nor a use. It has however been deducted from the profit to arrive at net profit and therefore needs to be added back to arrive at the profit figure for the funds statement.

1.3 Scott Ltd

Funds statement

Sources		£000s	
Net profit		36	
Depreciation	44		
Less: profit on sale	1	43	
Sale of plant and machinery		2	
Issue of shares		20	
New loan obtained		10	
Increase in creditors		11	
Decrease in debtors		2	124

Uses

Purchase of plant	125	
Short-term investments bought	2	
Increase in stock	27	
Dividends paid	3	
Taxation paid	15	172
Decrease in cash/bank		48

Workings

	Plant at cost	Depreciation	Disposal
At start	100	40	
Sold	40		40
-ditto-		39	39
Book value			1
Proceeds			2
Profit on sale	—	—	1
	60	1	
Bought	**125**		
Depreciation for year		**44**	
At the end	185	45	

	P&L account
At start	31
Net profit	**36**
	67
Taxation	− 16
Dividends	− 4
At the end	47

	Taxation	Dividends
At start	15	2
Paid in the year	− 15	− 3
	0	− 1
In the current year	16	4
At the end	16	3

The details in **bold italics** are the assumptions that these are the missing figures.

1.4

The following financial decisions taken by management during 19X3 can be identified:

1   to depreciate the plant;
2   to sell part of the plant;
3   to issue shares;
4   to obtain a further loan;
5   to pay an increased dividend;

6   to increase creditors;
7   to decrease debtors;
8   to purchase more plant;
9   to purchase short-term investments;
10   to increase stock;
11   to pay the tax liability;
12   to operate at a profit;
13   to plough back profits for growth;
14   to decrease the cash at bank and in hand;

Quite a comprehensive list! This text will be examining in some detail the issues involved in an attempt to improve the quality of the decision-making.

1.5 Robbins Ltd

Budgeted funds statement

Sources		£000s
Net profit		15
Depreciation: motor vehicles	5	
plant and machinery	13	18
Loss on sale of motor vehicle		1
Proceeds from sale of motor vehicle		3
Decrease in debtors		4
		41
Uses		
Purchase of: motor vehicle	11	
plant	17	
	28	
Dividend paid	4	
Increase in stock	8	
Decrease in creditors	7	
Loan repaid	5	52
Decrease in cash in hand and at bank		11

Workings

	Vehicles at cost	Depreciation	Disposal
At start	24	15	
Disposal	7		7
-ditto-		3	3
Book value			4
Proceeds			3
Loss on sale			1
	17	12	
Bought	11		
Depreciation for year		5	
At the end	28	17	

	Retained earnings	Dividends
At start	30	3
Net Profit	15	
	45	
Paid in the year		−3
Dividends		
Interim	1	+1
Proposed	−2	+2
Paid in year		−1
At the end	42	2

1.6 Scott Limited

Cash flow statement for the year ended 19X3

Net cash inflow from operating activities (a)		65
Returns on investment and servicing of finance		
Loan Interest (b)	?	
Dividends paid	3	(3)
Taxation paid		(15)
Investing activities		
Payments to acquire tangible fixed assets:		
Plant	125	
Proceeds from sale of plant	(2)	
Short-term investments (c)	2	
Net cash outflow from investing activities		(125)
Net cash outflow before financing		(78)
Financing activities:		
Issue of shares	20	
New Loan obtained	10	
Net cash inflow from financing		30
Decrease in cash and cash equivalents		(48)

Workings

(a)   Net cash inflow from operating activities

Net profit	36
Depreciation	44
Profit on sale	(1)
Increase in creditors	11
Decrease in debtors	2
Increase in stock	(27)
	65

(b)   Interest paid to lenders should be included here, but the figure cannot be ascertained from the available information.

(c) The short-term investments could, alternatively, have been included under cash equivalents.

CAPITAL GEARING

5.1

Business risk relates to the type of business that the enterprise is engaged in, such as changes in demand for the products or services being sold, the level of competition and the extent to which business activity fluctuates. Financial risk is the ability of the enterprise to meet its fixed charges arising from the use of loan capital and preference shares. These include interest charges on loans, preference dividends and sums set aside for the redemption of the loans and preference shares at the end of their life.

5.2

Gearing is the measurement of the extent to which a company is funded by loans and/or preference shares rather than shareholders' equity.

5.3

1

	A Plc	B Plc	C Plc
	£000s	£000s	£000s
Profit before interest	104	104	104
Less: interest (6% × 130)	–	–	7.8
	104	104	96.2
Less: tax (30%)	31.2	31.2	28.86
	72.8	72.8	67.34
Less: preference dividend (7%)	–	10.92	9.10
	72.8	61.88	58.24
Number of ordinary shares	520	364	260
EPS	14p	17p	22.4p

2   Note that the EPS increases as the gearing level increases, indicating that the gearing up policy adopted by C Plc (and to a lesser extent B Plc) is working to the advantage of their respective ordinary shareholders.

5.4 Billings Ltd

1

$$\frac{\text{Debentures}}{\text{All long-term finance}} = \frac{40}{100 + 50 + 40} = 21\%$$

The gearing appears to be moderate rather than highly geared.

2

Profits before interest	22.4
Less: interest (6% × 40)	2.4
Profit before tax	20.0
Less: tax at 30%	6.0
	14.0
Less: ordinary dividend (5% × 100)	5.0
Retained earnings	9.0

Interest cover $\dfrac{22.4}{2.4}$ = 9.3 times

The interest cover is quite high indicating that more debt could be taken on board.

3 Ordinary dividend cover $\dfrac{14}{5}$ = 2.8 times

The dividend is covered nearly 3 times indicating little chance of not paying a dividend.

4 Return on equity $\dfrac{20}{150}$ = 13.3%

Return on all long-term funds $\dfrac{22.4}{190}$ = 11.8%

Note: The return on all long-term funds is made up of the returns on lenders' funds and on shareholders' funds viz.

$$\dfrac{2.4}{40} + \dfrac{20}{150} = 11.8\%$$

5 EPS $\dfrac{14}{100}$ = 14p

6 Assuming that the £50,000 was obtained all in long-term loan, the following changes would occur:

(a) Gearing: $\dfrac{40 + 50}{100 + 50 + 40 + 50}$ = 37.5%

This is a significant change, increasing the percentage level of gearing by (37.5 − 20.0/20) = 87.5%

(b) Profit before tax and interest (as before)   £22.4
Return on additional funds
22.4/190 = 11.8% previously

11.8% × 50	5.9
	28.3
Less: interest (6% × 90)	5.4
Profit before tax	22.9
Less: tax (30% × 22.9)	6.87
Available for dividends/retentions	16.03

Interest cover:

$$\frac{28.3}{5.4} = 5.2 \text{ times}$$

A considerable reduction from previously but still well covered.

(c) Ordinary dividend cover:

$$\frac{16.03}{5.0} = 3.21 \text{ times}$$

Slightly better than before.

(d) Return on equity $\frac{22.9}{150} = 15.3\%$

Return on long-term funds $\frac{28.3}{240} = 11.8\%$

These are no worse than previously.

(e) EPS $\frac{16.03}{100} = 16.03\text{p}$

This is an improvement on the previous figure.

Overall, we have confirmation that the company should issue more loans, as the returns exceed their cost after taxation effects and the benefit accrues to the ordinary shareholders, which is indicated by the increase in the EPS.

THE COST OF CAPITAL

6.1

1 Cost of equity $\frac{D}{P} + g \quad \frac{0.87}{4.35} + 5\% = 25\%$

2 Cost of debt $9\% - (30\% \times 9) = 6.3\%$

6.2

Workings

1   The market price per ordinary share is:

$$\frac{£120,000}{80,000} = £1.50$$

2   The market value of the loan stock is:

$75\% \times £40,000 = £30,000$

The interest payable is:

$6\% \times £40,000 = £2,400$

The rate of interest is therefore:

$$\frac{2,400}{30,000} \times 100 = 8\%$$

i.e. $8\% \times £30,000 = £2,400$, the same as 6% on £40,000.

The prevailing interest rate must have increased, thus forcing down the market value of the stock. The same *amount* of interest is paid regardless.
The calculation of the WACC is as follows:

	(2) £000s	(3) Gross	(4) Tax	(5) After tax	(6) (2) × (5)
Loan stock	30	8%	3.2%	4.8%	1.44k
Equity	120	17%*		17.0%	20.40k
	150				21.84k

$$\text{WACC } \frac{21.84}{150.00} = 14.56\%$$

$$\frac{*£0.15}{£1.50} + 7\% = 17\%$$

Note that the reserves are part of equity and they are effectively included in the market value of the shares so no further inclusion is required.

6.3

The calculation of the WACC is as follows:

	(2) £000s	(3) Gross	(4) Tax	(5) After tax	(6) (2) × (5)
Loan stock	30	8%	3.2%	4.8%	1.44k
Add'l loan	50	9%	3.6%	5.4%	2.70k
Equity	96	21.4%*		21.4%	20.544k
	176				24.684k

$$\text{WACC}\ \frac{24.684}{176.00} = 14.03\%$$

$$\frac{*£0.18}{£1.25} + 7\% = 21.4\%$$

6.4

The WACC has gone down from 14.56 per cent to 14.03 per cent, which indicates that the introduction of the extra loan stock, with an after tax cost of 5.4 per cent has more than compensated for the increase in the cost of equity from 17.0 per cent to 21.4 per cent. The stock market has compensated for the extra risk to the ordinary shareholders, reflected in the demand for the shares, by reducing the share price from £1.50 to £1.25. The increased level of gearing has proved beneficial to the company measured by the fall in the weighted average cost of capital.

6.5

Both 1 and 2 have the same effect: the gearing level is reduced. If the stock market perceives this as good, then the share price will rise. An increase in the share price, with the other variables constant, will reduce the cost of equity. However, that reduction may not be sufficient to avoid an increase in the WACC due to the disappearance of the after tax lower cost of debt.

INTRODUCTION TO THE THEORY OF OPTIMAL GEARING

7.1

$$\begin{aligned}\text{Using RRR} &= i + (\bar{R}m - i)\,B \\ &= 4 + (12 - 4)\ 1.25 \\ &= 14\%\end{aligned}$$

7.2

1

Honley Plc

$$\text{EPS} = £2\ \text{million} - \text{tax}\ £0.5\ \text{million} = £1.5\ \text{million}\quad £1.5\text{m}/£3.0\text{m} = £0.50$$

As all available profits are distributed then the EPS is the same as the dividend per share.

$$\text{Cost of equity (i.e. Ke)} = \frac{£0.50}{£2.50} + 0\ \text{growth} = 20\%$$

WACC = 20% (the same as equity as there is no gearing)

Garforth Plc

EBIT	£2.0m
Less: debenture interest	0.12
Net profit	1.88
Less: tax @ 25%	0.47
	1.41

$$\text{EPS} = \frac{£1.41\,\text{m}}{1.7625} = £0.80$$

$$\text{Ke} = \frac{£0.80}{£3.20} + 0 \text{ growth} = 25\%$$

WACC

Equity 1.7625 m × £3.20 = £5.64 m   25% – tax = 25%   £1.41 m

Debentures 2 m × 75p* = $\dfrac{£1.50\,\text{m}}{£7.14\,\text{m}}$ 8% – tax = 6% $\dfrac{£0.09\,\text{m}}{£1.50\,\text{m}}$

$$\frac{£1.50\,\text{m}}{£7.14\,\text{m}} = 21\%$$

$$\frac{*0.06}{0.08} = 75\,\text{p}$$

2 (a) The cost of equity is higher in Garforth due to the increased *financial risk* by that company gearing up.

 (b) The WACC is also higher in Garforth indicating that the company is too highly geared under the prevailing circumstances.

3 The yield on equity after tax is:

	Honley	Garforth
Net profit	£2.0 m	£1.88m
Tax	0.5 m	0.47m
	1.5 m	1.41 m
Value of equity	3 m shares × £2.50 = £7.5 m	1.7625 shares × £3.20 = £5.64 m
Yield on equity	1.5/7.5 = 20%	1.41/5.64 = 25%
Yield on debentures		6% on £2 m or 8% on £1.5 m

4 Mr Lister's income is:

2,000/1,762,500 × £1.41m = £1,600

5 The gearing level of Garforth is:

150/564 = 26.6% approx.

He needs to borrow:

0.266 × 2,000 = 532

NB He sells 2,000 for cash

borrows $\dfrac{532}{2,532}$

532/2,532 = 21% which is the same as 150/714

6   If he invests in Honley his income will be:

$\dfrac{2,532}{3,000,000}$ × £2m =   £1,688.00

Less: borrowed 10% × 532 $\dfrac{53.20}{£1,634.80}$

This is better than the £1,600 he is currently getting from his investment in Garforth.

7   The action described above is the 'arbitrage process'.

7.3

Queensgate Plc

1
% level of debt	% cost of debt (after tax)	% level of equity	% cost of equity	% WACC
0	8	100	18	18.0
10	8	90	18	17.0
20	9	80	18	16.2
30	10	70	20	17.0
40	12	60	22	18.0
50	14	50	24	19.0
60	17	40	27	21.0
70	25	30	35	28.0

2   See graph opposite.
3   The cost of equity (Ke) rises with the increased gearing due to the increased required rate of return demanded by the ordinary shareholders caused by their higher financial risk. The cost of debt (Kd) rises with the increased gearing due to the increased financial risk to the lenders. The WACC falls (traditional view) then rises beyond the optimal level which is where the WACC is minimized.
4   The optimal level is at the 20 per cent level of debt with the WACC at 16.2 per cent.

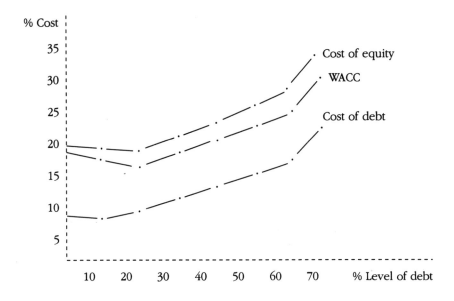

5   $Ke = 5\% + (18 - 5)\ 1.0 = 18\%$ as in (1) above where the gearing level is zero. Therefore:

$35\% = 5\% + (18 - 5)\ B$
$B = 2.3077$

Beta rises from 1.0 to 2.3077 due to the increased financial risk caused by the high level of gearing. Therefore we are able to conclude that the Beta measures the volatility of risk.

7.4

The list should include such items as indicated below:

1   The importance of risk and the reward for it. The reward is lower for debt and therefore the excess returns accrue to the benefit of the ordinary shareholders.
2   The effect on the WACC. It lowers it initially, though it will rise with increased levels of gearing.
3   With the lower WACC more capital projects become available.
4   The cheapest source of finance is used to finance capital projects.
5   The use of debt avoids the dilution of capital.
6   Default on debt may cause the loss of control by the appointment of a receiver.
7   In inflationary periods, debt will be redeemed with £s of a different value.
8   Debt in the capital structure is not liked by a takeover bidder and may act as part of a useful defensive strategy.

CAPITAL INVESTMENT APPRAISAL

8.1

The average cash inflow is 45,000/5   = £9,000
The average depreciation is 30,000/5   = £6,000
The average accounting profit is 9,000 − 6,000 = £3,000
The average capital employed is 30,000/2   = £15,000
The accounting rate of return is 3,000/15,000 = 20%

8.2

£21,000 paid back after 2 years, and £31,000 paid back after 3 years. Therefore the payback period is:

2 years + (9,000/10,000) = 2 years 10.8 months

8.3

			Discounted cash flow (DCF)	Cumulative
Year 1	8,000	0.870	6,960	6,960
Year 2	20,000	0.756	15,120	22,080
Year 3	14,000	0.658	9,212	31,292
Year 4	6,000	0.572	3,432	34,724

The discounted payback period is:

3 years + 708/9,212 × 365 = 3 years 28 days

Note that by increasing the discount rate, the cash flows are reduced, thus extending the payback period.

8.4

			Discounted cash flow (DCF)
Year 1	8,000	0.870	6,960
Year 2	20,000	0.756	15,120
Year 3	14,000	0.658	9,212
Year 4	6,000	0.572	3,432
			34,724
Less: initial cost			32,000
NPV			2,724

At a cost of capital of 15 per cent the project is still acceptable.

8.5

	10%		12%	
15,000	0.909	13,635	0.893	13,395
20,000	0.826	16,520	0.797	15,940
7,000	0.751	5,257	0.712	4,984
		35,412		34,319

Total range = 1,093
Excess over cost = 412

1   IRR = 10% + ((412/1,093) × 2) = 10.75%
2   At 10% cost of capital, the NPV is £412
3   As the IRR exceeds the 10% cost of capital the project is worthwhile. The NPV is positive and under this rule the project should be accepted.

INTRODUCTION TO RISK IN CAPITAL BUDGETING

9.1

By increasing the discount rate, the NPV is reduced. If it becomes negative the project would not be acceptable. Therefore the higher the risk premium the greater the chance that the project will not be acceptable.

9.2

The coefficient of variation is:

300/4,000 = 0.075

9.3

	Project B		
Probability	*DCF*		
0.10	£2,000	=	200
0.20	3,000	=	600
0.40	3,500	=	1,400
0.20	5,500	=	1,100
0.10	6,000	=	600
	Expected value		3,900

9.4

1 (a)

Brand EM				Brand Super EM		
3,000	0.10	300		1,000	0.10	100
4,000	0.25	1,000		2,000	0.25	500
5,000	0.30	1,500		3,000	0.30	900
6,000	0.25	1,500		4,000	0.25	1000
7,000	0.10	700		5,000	0.10	500
	Expected value	5,000			Expected value	3,000

(b)

Co-efficient of variation:

$$\frac{1,140}{5,000} = 0.228 \qquad \frac{1,140}{3,000} = 0.380$$

2   Super EM has the greater risk having a lower expected value and a greater co-efficient of variation, even though both proposals have the same standard deviation.

9.5

$$RRR = 0.03 + (0.12 - 0.03) \times 1.3$$
$$= 0.03 + 0.117$$
$$= 14.7\%$$

As the expected return is 18%, an excess of 3.3%, the project should be undertaken.

LEASES AND LEASING

10.5

Lease versus buy decision

Buying	Capital allowances computation			
Year	Cost/written down value b/f	Writing down allowance @ 25%	Tax @ 30%	Written down value c/f
	£	£	£	£
1	320,000	80,000	24,000	240,000
2	240,000	60,000	18,000	180,000
3	180,000	45,000	13,500	135,000
4	135,000			
Residual value	160,000			
	25,000	Balancing charge	(£7,500)	

Buying Year	Cost	Tax relief	Net cash flow	Present value factor @ 10%	Present value
	£	£	£	£	£
0	(320,000)				(320,000)
1		—	—	0.90909	—
2		24,000	24,000	0.82645	19,835
3		18,000	18,000	0.75131	13,524
4	128,000	13,500	141,500	0.68301	96,646
5		(7,500)	(7,500)	0.62092	(4,657)
					(£194,652)

Leasing

Year	Lease payment	Tax relief @ 30%	Net cash flow	Present value factor @ 10%	Present value
	£	£	£	£	£
0	(84,000)	—	(84,000)	—	(84,000)
1	(84,000)	—	(84,000)	0.90909	(76,364)
2	(84,000)	25,200	(58,800)	0.82645	(48,595)
3	(84,000)	25,200	(58,800)	0.75131	(44,177)
4	128,000 share of residual value	25,200	153,200	0.68301	104,637
5		25,200			
	Tax on residual value	(38,400)	(13,200)	0.62092	(8,196)
					(£156,695)

In this particular case leasing costs quite a bit less than buying outright. However, this information is just one piece of information which needs to be viewed in conjunction with other data before a final decision is made, even though on the basis of these figures it seems to be quite clear that the lease is the best option.

DIVIDEND POLICY

12.1

The payout ratio is

900/3,000 = 0.30 or

Dividend per share: 900/10,000 = 0.09

Earnings per share: 3,000/10,000 = 0.30

0.09/0.30 = 0.30

12.2

The answer to this question is contained within the chapter but may be classified as internal factors and external factors.

12.3

The implications for a company which had a dividend payout of 90 per cent, would be that it would have insufficient internal funds for investment projects. This might suggest that the company was not generating any worthwhile projects. On the other hand, if it was, it would have to look to its shareholders to provide the funds by way of a rights issue, which would prove more costly than retaining the funds in the first place. There is also the risk that the funds might not be forthcoming. The short-term benefits of a possible increase in share price, could therefore be offset by a shortage of funds for investment in the long term.

SHARE VALUATION

13.1

Equity is comprised of the issued ordinary share capital plus all the reserves of the company.

13.2 Townend Ltd

Net assets value

Premises (substituting current value)	£0.76m
Motor vehicles	0.50
Stock	0.40
Debtors	0.60
Bank	0.02
	2.28
Less: creditors	0.48
Net assets	1.80

Net assets value = 1.8m/0.2m shares = £9 each

Value based on dividends

Dividend per share = £0.12m/0.2m shares = 60p

Value based on dividends = 0.60p/0.075 = £8 each

Value based on earnings

Earnings per share = £0.24m/0.2m shares = £1.20

Value based on earnings = £1.2 × 9 = £10.80

13.3

The controlling interest would be worth something in excess the basic valuations. As the valuations calculated are £9, £8 and £10.80 respectively, it is suggested that his interest would be closer to the higher valuation of £10.80.

13.4 Laurel Ltd

Dividend per share	= (6% × 200,000)/200,000	= 6p per share
Value per share	= 0.06/0.08	= 75p per share
Check:		
Current value	= 200,000 × 75p	= £150,000
Dividend	= 6% × 200,000	= £12,000
Return on investment	= 12,000/150,000	= 8%

MERGERS AND TAKEOVERS

1
17.1

Refer to the text in Chapter 17 for the answer to this question.

17.2

A Plc		*B Plc*	
£1.25		£0.75	
× 2 =	2.50	× 3 =	2.25
× 3 =	3.75	× 5 =	3.75

The offer should be 3 shares in A Plc for 5 in B Plc.

17.3

Refer to the text in Chapter 17 for the answer to this question.

17.4

Using the dividend yield of Urban Plc, the value per share in Rural Ltd becomes:

$$0.30/0.075 = £4.00$$

Using the P/E ratio of Urban Plc, the value per share in Rural Ltd based on earnings becomes:

$$9 × £0.50 = £4.50$$

2	*Urban Plc*		*Rural Ltd*	
	£2.25		£4.50	
	× 2	4.50	× 1	4.50

The offer could be two shares in Urban Plc for one in Rural Ltd. This would value Rural Ltd at £4.50p per share, i.e. the value based on earnings.

17.5

Refer to the text in Chapter 17 for the answer to this question.

FINANCIAL NUMERACY

A.1

(a) £1,300 × 6% × 5 years =£1,300 × 30% = £390 interest

$$1,300 + 390 = £1,690$$

Note: Where i = interest, P = principal (i.e. the initial investment)

$r\%$ = interest rate per annum
n = the number of years
S = the total sum

then $i = r \times P \times n$
and $S = P + i$ (or $P + rPn$)
then $S = P(1 + rn)$

(b)   Using the above formulae:

$i = 7\% \times £4,000 \times 3$ years $= £840$
$S = £4,000(1 + 7\% \times 3) = £4,840$

(c)   Using the above formula $S = P(1 + rn)$

$£1,080 = P(1 + 5\% \times 4\text{yrs}) = P(1.20)$
$P = 1,080/1.20$
$P = £900$

A.2

(a) At start	£1,300
6% × £1,300	£78
End of year 1	1,378
6% × £1,378 (say)	83
End of year 2	1,461
6% × £1,461 (say)	88
End of year 3	1,549
6% × £1,549 (say)	93
End of year 4	1,642
6% × £1,642 (say)	98
End of year 5	1,740

Note: Where:

i = interest, P = principal (i.e. the initial investment)
$r\%$ = interest rate per annum
n = the number of years
S = the total sum

then at end of:

first year $S = £1,378$ or $S1 = P(1 + r/100)$
second year $S = £1,461$ or $S2 = P(1 + r/100)^2$
third year $S = £1,549$ or $S3 = P(1 + r/100)^3$
fourth year $S = £1,642$ or $S4 = P(1 + r/100)^4$
fifth year $S = £1,740$ or $S5 = P(1 + r/100)^5$

so: $S = P(1 + r/100)^n$

(b) Using the formula in A.2(a):

$S = £4,000(1 + 0.06)^3$
$ = 4,000(1.191016)$
$ = £4,764$

The total interest is $£764$
The total paid is $£4,764$

(c) Using the formula in 2(a):

$1,489 = P(1 + 5/100)^4$
$1,489 = P(1.2155)$
$ P = 1,489/1.2155$
$ P = £1,225$

A.3

Now	£2,000			
Yr 1 Int	160			
	2,160	£2,000		
Yr 2 Int	173	160		
	2,333	2,160	£2,000	
Yr 3 Int	186	173	160	
	2,519	2,333	2,160	= £7,012

There will be $£7,012$ available for the purchase.

This can be explained as follows. If $£D$ is deposited at the beginning of each of t years at a compound interest rate of $r\%$, then the sum accrued, $£S$, at the end of t years can be expressed:

$£S = £D(R(R^t - 1)/(R - 1))$ where $R = (1 + r/100)$

Thus $£S = £2,000(1.08(1.08^3 - 1)/(1.08 - 1))$
$\qquad = £2,000(1.08(0.259712)/(0.08))$
$\qquad = £2,000(1.08)(3.2464)$
$\qquad = £7,012$

(b) Using the above formula:

$\quad £S = £1,500(1.07(1.07^4 - 1)/(1.07 - 1))$
$\qquad = £1,500(1.07(1.310796 - 1)/(0.07))$
$\qquad = £1,500(1.07(4.4399))$
$\qquad = £7,126$

A.4

(a) Refer to the principles of discounting in Chapter 8. It can be seen that $100/(1 + 10)^2 = 0.826$ – being the discount factor. The formula shown is:

$\quad P = S/(1 + r)^n$

$\quad$ Therefore $P = £25,000/(1 + 0.10)^2$
$\qquad\qquad\quad = £25,000/1.21$
$\qquad\qquad\quad = £20,661$ approx.

Note that dividing S by 1.21 is the same as multiplying by $1/1.21$, i.e. 0.8264.

(b) Using the above formula:

$\quad P = £12,000/(1 + 0.08)^3$
$\qquad = £12,000/1.259712$
$\qquad = £9,526$

$\quad$ Note that $1/1.259712 = 0.7938$
$\quad$ and $£12,000 \times 0.7938 = £9,526$

Also by reference to the present value tables in Appendix 3 you will see that for year 3 and 8 per cent interest rate, the discount factor is 0.794 after rounding.

A.5

(a) $\quad £D = £1,375 \quad R = 1.10 \quad t = 5$ years

Using the formula

$\quad £S = £D((R^t - 1)/(rR^t))$

$\quad £S = £1,375 ((1.10^5 - 1)/(0.10 \times 1.10^5))$
$\qquad = £1,375 (0.61051/0.161051)$
$\qquad = £1,375 (3.790786)$
$\qquad = £5,212$

When the present value of £5,212 is compared with the initial investment of £6,000, it can be seen that the investment is not worthwhile.

Note: The same answer is calculated where the cumulative present value tables are used viz.:

Reading off at 5 years at 10% = 3.791

$$3.791 \times £1,375 = £5,212$$

(b)

$$£6,000 = £D((1.10^5 - 1) (0.10 \times 1.10^5))$$
$$£D = £6,000/3.790786$$
$$= £1,582.79$$

The minimum amount acceptable as the annuity payment is £1,582.79.

Appendix 5

Glossary of terms

Accounts payable and receivable Sums owed to or receivable from creditors and debtors respectively.

Annuity A sum of money paid regularly to a person called an annuitant either for a fixed period of time or until specific person (usually the annuitant) dies.

Beta coefficient Another term for a regression coefficient, used to measure the volatility of risk.

Bonus issue Also called a capitalization issue, is an issue of bonus shares by transferring realized or unrealized profits to the share capital account.

Capital budgeting The process of choosing, from a number of possible investment opportunities, the ones in which to invest.

Capital expenditure Expenditure on fixed assets.

Capital structure The proportions of the capital of an enterprise that are derived from each of its various sources of capital.

Cash budget An estimate of the monetary receipts and payments of an enterprise over a future period showing when it will be necessary to borrow money and when there will be surplus money available for investment.

Cash discount Part of the invoiced charge that will be cancelled if payment for the invoice is received within a specified period of time.

Cash flow The pattern and extent of receipts and payments of money by an enterprise over a period of time. Receipts and payments are cash inflows and outflows respectively.

Credit rating An assessment of how freely credit should be extended to an existing or prospective customer.

Current asset An asset of an enterprise not intended for use on a continuing basis in the enterprise's activities. It is one that is capable of providing funds from which liabilities arising from the ordinary activities of the enterprise can be met.

Debt factoring The sale of trade debts to a factor whereby the factor collects payment of the debts. The factor often maintains the debtor's ledger on behalf of clients. See also *Invoice discounting*.

Distributable profits Profits available for distribution as dividends to shareholders.

Dividend An amount of the company's profits payable to its shareholders.

Earnings per share The profit of a company for a period after deducting tax and dividends to preference shareholders, divided by the number of issued ordinary shares eligible for dividend.

Enterprise Something which is a party to financial transactions and for which accounting records are kept relating only to its transactions.

Equity capital Capital contributed by the ordinary shareholders of a company plus all the reserves to which they are legally entitled.

Fixed asset An asset of an enterprise intended for use on a continuing basis.

Gearing Financing the operations of an enterprise with money on which only a fixed rate of interest or dividend is payable in the expectation that income from the operations thus financed will be greater than the fixed interest or dividends payable and the difference will accrue for the benefit of the owners of the business.

Group A parent company and its subsidiaries.

Insolvency The inability of a person or enterprise to pay legally incurred debts as they fall due.

Interim dividend A dividend paid by a company to its members during a financial year and regarded as a part payment of the total dividend for that year.

Invoice discounting The sale by an enterprise of debts owed to that enterprise without informing the debtors of the sale. The enterprise collects payment of the debts on behalf of the purchaser. See also *Debt factoring*.

Member In a company which is limited by shares, a member is an ordinary shareholder.

Net assets The total assets of an enterprise less its total liabilities (which include long-term loans and provisions).

Net current assets The value of the current assets minus the value of the current liabilities at a particular point in time. Also known as working capital.

Net present value The total of the present values of amounts receivable minus the total of the present values of the amounts payable.

Net worth Another term for owner equity.

Operating profit The profit of an accounting period derived from the ordinary activities of an enterprise and calculated without deducting interest on long-term loans, preference dividends and taxation.

Overtrading Expansion of the sales and production of a business without adequate financial support.

Payback period The length of time necessary for the returns on an investment to equal the initial sum invested.

Present value The value now, of a sum of money to be received or paid at some future date. The rate of interest used in the calculation is called the discount rate.

Price/earnings ratio (P/E ratio) The market price of an equity share of a company quoted on the Stock Exchange, divided by the company's earnings per share.

Ratio analysis   Assessment of the performance of an organization by calculating ratios and noting how these alter over time or in comparing them with
the same measures calculated for other organizations.

Rights issue   An issue of shares in a company which are offered to existing
shareholders with each member being offered a number of shares which will
maintain that shareholder's proportionate holding in the company.

Window dressing   Carrying out artificial transactions which will later have to
be reversed, in order to improve temporarily the financial position shown by
the financial statements, without disclosing that the position will later be
reversed.

INDEX